'Nicolson writes with authority on the Bloomsbury Group, and ... gives a thorough and illuminating account of the Woolfs' publishing business, the Hogarth Press, and makes a persuasive case for Woolf's "excellence as a traveller" ... Broadly appreciative and admirably concise'
Susanna Rustin, *Financial Times*

'His affectionate, but not uncritical study is a valuable corrective to some of the more hysterical American feminist critics ... Nicolson is fascinating on Woolf's breakdowns, snobbery, xenophobia, lack of political engagement and even her sex life' *Sunday Times*

'Can there be any justification for an extra book? The answer, rather surprisingly, is a decisive yes. What other book about Virginia Woolf begins with her hunting butterflies with the author? ... [Nicolson] writes clearly and with fair-mindedness, weighing up feminist theory, medical speculation and cultural analysis' Michael Holroyd, *Mail on Sunday*

'*Virginia Woolf* ... says all you need to know about the modernist, feminist icon in 165 pages ... If only all literary lives were as succinct' *Time Out*

'Nigel Nicolson's *Virginia Woolf* is poised between biography and memoir, and infused by the author's personal reminiscences, which are warm but clear-sighted. A sense of balance is conferred by Nicolson's close connection with the social and intellectual *milieux* within which Woolf lived and worked. There is an understanding here which goes beyond what may be derived simply from research in university archives ... what the book conveys, above all, is the texture of the friendships that influenced her writing. As Bloomsbury recedes from living memory, there is a tendency for what was a diverse group of friends to congeal, in the popular imagination, into a movement, whose contribution to 20th-century culture can be summarised in some facile way. Nicolson's study is a valuable corrective' *Church Times*

'... modest, affectionate but clear-eyed book about the woman he grew up regarding as a favourite aunt ... Nigel Nicolson was the perfect choice to write this study of Virginia Woolf ... As Nicolson says of Virginia Woolf's own biography of Roger Fry, it is "alternately taut with meaning and running fresh with pleasure" ' Anne Chisholm, *Spectator*

'This is an unusual (and unusually charming) biography ... It is a quality of wide-eyed observation that gives this book its charm. Woolf comes alive in it ... vivid vignettes are the essence of Nicolson's book ... Nicolson's personal re-collections run like a silver thread through this biography. But he tells the whole story of Woolf's life with authority – affectionately but not uncritically. He is especially good at describing the trance-like states which went to the writing of Woolf's best novels' Robert Nye, *Scotsman*

'Nicolson makes good use of his privileged access to his subject ... Nicolson's snatches of memory are particularly valuable when they smack up hard against the authorised version ... nothing beats the excitement of feeling that you're in the presence of someone who once walked with giants ... Nigel Nicolson's recollections of the woman whom he regarded "like a favourite aunt" are to be recom-mended' Kathryn Hughes, *Daily Telegraph*

Nigel Nicolson was born in 1917, the son of two well-known British writers, Harold Nicolson and Vita Sackville-West. He has written several biographies, including that of this parents, *Portrait of a Marriage*, and *Mary Curzon* (which won the Whitbread Prize), as well as books on politics and the arts. He was Editor of the six volumes of Virginia Woolf's letters. For some years he was a Member of Parliament, and is co-founder of the publishing firm of Weidenfeld & Nicolson. He lives at Sissinghurst Castle in Kent, now a property of the National Trust. He was awarded the OBE for 'service to literature and to the historic environment' in the Queen's Birthday Honours, June 2000.

By Nigel Nicolson

Vita and Harold
Portrait of a Marriage
Mary Curzon
Long Life: Memoirs
Virginia Woolf

VIRGINIA
WOOLF

NIGEL NICOLSON

PHŒNIX

A PHOENIX PAPERBACK

First published in Great Britain in 2000
by Weidenfeld & Nicolson
This paperback edition published in 2001
by Phoenix,
an imprint of Orion Books Ltd,
Orion House, 5 Upper St Martin's Lane,
London WC2H 9EA

A CIP catalogue record for this book
is available from the British Library.

ISBN 0 75381 147 2

Typeset by Selwood Systems, Midsomer Norton

Printed and bound in Great Britain by
Butler & Tanner Ltd, Frome and London

to Joanne Trautmann Banks

ILLUSTRATIONS

* Courtesy of the National Portrait Gallery.
All other photographs from the author's collection.

ACKNOWLEDGEMENTS

I wish to thank Ed Victor, my literary agent, for suggesting this book to me and for much other help, and the following for permission to quote from Virginia Woolf's published books, diaries, letters and some unpublished papers:

The Society of Authors, as the Literary Representative of the Estate of Virginia Woolf, and Olivier Bell, the editor of her Diaries.

The Berg Collection of English and American Literature, the New York Public Library (Astor, Lenox and Tilden Foundations).

Quotations from other books listed in the Bibliography are acknowledged in the text, and covered by the 'fair dealing' convention which permits short quotations without specific consent from the authors, to whom I owe my thanks.

I thank Ms Sue Fox for much help and advice.

N.N.

January 2000

I

IN HER CHILDHOOD Virginia Woolf was a keen hunter of butterflies and moths. With her brothers and sister she would smear tree trunks with treacle to attract and capture the insects, and then pin their lifelike corpses to cork boards, their wings outspread. It was an interest that persisted into her adult life, and when she discovered that I too was a bug-hunter, she insisted that we go hunting together in the fields around Long Barn, our house in Kent, two miles from Knole, my mother's birthplace. I was nine years old.

One summer's afternoon when we were sweeping the tall grass with our nets and catching nothing, she suddenly paused, leaning on her bamboo cane as a savage might lean on his assegai, and said to me: 'What's it like to be a child?' I, taken aback, replied, 'Well, Virginia, you know what it's like. You've been a child yourself. I don't know what it's like to be you, because I've never been grown-up.' It was the only occasion when I got the better of her, dialectically.

I believe that her motive was to gather copy for her portrait of James in *To the Lighthouse*, which she was writing at the time, and James was about my own age. She told me that it was not much use thinking back into her own childhood, because little girls are different from little boys. 'But were you happy as a child?', I asked.

I forget what she replied, but now I think I know the answer, since her childhood and youth have been more amply recorded than almost any other. It was not so much unhappy, as troubled. Her mother died when she was thirteen, and her half-sister when she was fifteen. At twenty-two she lost her father, and two years later her brother Thoby. Another half-sister was mentally deranged. Virginia herself, while still quite young, suffered from periods of acute depression and even insanity. She was sexually abused by her half-brothers when she was too young to understand what was happening. It was a string of calamities that could have resulted in a youth that was deeply disturbed. But she was courageous, resilient and enterprising. As her early letters and diaries reveal more convincingly than her later recollections, she developed normally enough, and although she was indifferent to social success, she had a gift for friendship, and very early in her life, an impulse to turn every experience into words. It was on the same occasion as our butterfly hunt that she said to me, 'Nothing has really happened until it has been described. So you must write many letters to your family and friends, and keep a diary.' Pain was relieved, and pleasure doubled, by recording it.

Virginia was born in London on 25 January 1882, the third child of Leslie and Julia Stephen. For both her parents it was a second marriage, and each partner inherited from the other, children born of the first. It is simpler to describe their complex genealogy by a diagram, to which I have added in brackets their ages in 1895, the year when Julia died:

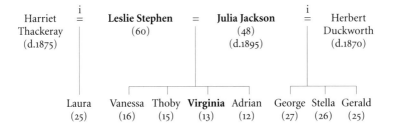

Harriet	i	**Leslie Stephen**	=	**Julia Jackson**	i	Herbert
Thackeray	=	(60)		(48)	=	Duckworth
(d.1875)				(d.1895)		(d.1870)

Laura	Vanessa	Thoby	**Virginia**	Adrian	George	Stella	Gerald
(25)	(16)	(15)	(13)	(12)	(27)	(26)	(25)

Laura was the mentally unbalanced child, who was treated by her father with scant affection, and after Julia's death was placed by him in a mental home where she lived until she died at the age of seventy-five. Leslie's first wife, a daughter of William Thackeray, the novelist, and Julia's first husband, Herbert Duckworth, a handsome barrister, can have meant little to Virginia apart from the tragedy of their early deaths and the progeny of cousins, chiefly Fishers and Vaughans, which they generated. It was a large family group, from which different members entered Virginia's life with varying degrees of intimacy and persistence. Emma and Madge Vaughan (the original of Sally in *Mrs Dalloway*) were among her earliest friends, but they were not to last long in her affections.

The people who mattered most to her in childhood were her parents, her sister Vanessa and her elder brother Thoby. Julia was the daughter of John Jackson, who spent much of his career as a doctor in Calcutta, and Maria Pattle. Like her mother, Julia was one of the most beautiful women of her age.

In her youth she posed for Watts, Burne-Jones, and her aunt Julia Margaret Cameron, the photographer, who has left an image of her which is distinctly Pre-Raphaelite, often tragic in countenance, and like Virginia, always beautiful but never pretty. What strikes one most about these portraits is the serenity of her gaze, as if life was a constant test of character which she would survive triumphantly, but this impression may be due to the immobility needed for early photography: one cannot hold a smile longer than an instant without it appearing false. In *To the Lighthouse*, where Mrs Ramsay is a close portrait of Julia, Virginia shows us another side of her mother's character – swift, decisive, impatient of stupidity, quick-tempered but incapable of unkindness. In a memoir dated 1907 she wrote of her parents, 'Beautiful often, even to our eyes, were their gestures, their glances of pure and unutterable delight in each other.'   Leslie revered Julia, and she controlled him by her submissiveness. In a sense she was the stronger character of the two, quietly dominating. But Leslie was no weakling. Born the son of Sir James Stephen, a senior civil servant and then a Professor of history, he developed from a shy boy into a man who could be formidable, and as a mountaineer, tough. He was ordained a clergyman in his youth but lost his faith and left Cambridge for London, where he earned his living as a literary and political journalist, and became a leading intellectual, the originator and first editor of *The Dictionary of National Biography*, a friend of Meredith, Hardy, Henry James, Tennyson, Matthew Arnold and George Eliot.   Virginia's childhood was therefore comfortably upper-middle-class and intellectually stimulating. They lived in a respectable Kensington cul-de-sac, 22 Hyde

Virginia Woolf in 1902, when she was 20. A studio photograph by George Beresford. Like her mother, Julia Stephen, Virginia was 'always beautiful, but never pretty'.

Park Gate, where seven servants ran the house under Julia's directions. The weekly journal, *Hyde Park Gate News*, which Virginia and Vanessa began in 1891 and sustained for four years, portrays a lively, talented, funny family, in which tensions were cushioned by mutual affection. The older members supported the younger, and the younger amused their elders. Virginia's talent for fiction developed early. When she was only six or seven, she wrote to her mother (the letter first surfaced in Joanne Trautmann Banks's *Congenial Spirits*):

> Mrs Prinsep says that she will only go in a slow train cos she says all the fast trains have accidents and she told us about an old man of 70 who got his legs caute in the weels of the train and the train began to go on and the old gentleman was draged along till the train caute fire and he called out for somebody to cut off his legs but nobody came he was burnt up. Goodbye. Your loving Virginia.

The legend that Leslie was cantankerous and indifferent to his children is not confirmed by the many references to them in his letters to Julia, now in the Berg Collection, New York Public Library. He called them his ragamice, and Virginia was Ginia: 'Kiss my ragamice and Ginia. There will be no more of that breed.' 'Little Ginia is already an accomplished flirt. I said today that I must go down to my work. She nestled herself down on the sofa by me, squeezed her little self tightly up against me, and then gazed up with her bright eyes through her shock of hair and said, "Don't go, papa". She looked full of mischief all the time. I never saw such a little rogue.' 'My sweet little Ginia. I shall be glad to have her back.' 'My love to all my pets, specially my Ginia. I have been thinking of her all day.' 'Ginia tells me a story every night.' And then this, when Virginia was eleven: 'Yesterday I discussed George III with her. She takes in a great deal, and will really be an author in time.'

Their holidays were spent in Cornwall, at St Ives, where Leslie rented Talland House for thirteen summers until Julia died. It was a curious choice for a man who was not naturally a beachcomber, and was careful with his money. Cornwall was distant from London, and the expense of transporting his large family and several servants was considerable. When they had recovered from the long journey, the children were very happy there, and Leslie showed his kindest side, relaxed and paternal. Two years before her death Virginia wrote, 'St Ives gave me all the pure delight which is before my eyes, even at this moment'. Every day brought an experience which, if not novel, was treated as a novelty – walking on the moors, swimming, boating, shopping, and playing games, indoor and out. A photograph taken in Cornwall when she was about six shows Virginia sturdy, tomboyish, concentrating on her role as wicket-keeper while Adrian batted. Then an incident occurred that was to surface years later in one of her best-loved novels. She recorded it in *Hyde Park Gate News*: 'Master Adrian Stephen was much disappointed at not being allowed to go.' It was the expedition to Godrevy lighthouse in St Ives Bay.

When Julia died, life changed for all of them. They found no consolation in religion. Both Virginia's parents were agnostic. Though their children had 'sponsors', none of them were baptized. Leslie was exhausted by his grief, and by the tide of relations who washed up at Hyde Park Gate to gratify their benevolence and overwhelm him with excessive sympathy. He would groan aloud at meals, and complain every week when Stella, who had taken on her mother's role as housekeeper, presented the weekly bills for payment. 'He went through an extraordinary dramatisation of self-pity', Virginia wrote in recollection. 'He sank into his chair and sat with his head on his breast. At last, after glancing at a book, he would look up and say half-plaintively, "And what are you doing this afternoon, Ginny?" Never have I felt such rage and such frustration.'

He was in danger of losing his children's affection. They felt imprisoned by him. The boys could escape to school, but the girls were housebound. When Stella fell in love with Jack Hills, Leslie's attitude was like that of Mr Woodhouse in *Emma*, thinking only that he would be deprived of her company and help, and when she married, his only consolation was that they took a house across the street. When Stella died, probably of peritonitis, only three months after her wedding, he seemed not particularly to mind. His capacity for grief had been exhausted by Julia's death, and Vanessa could take over the management of the house, which she did, dutifully and reluctantly.

In later life Virginia would sometimes complain that she was denied the education that was given automatically to boys, but her protests were not consistent nor wholly justified. Once, in middle age, she wrote to Vita Sackville-West, who had reproached her for her lack of 'jolly vulgarity', that she had had no chance to acquire it. 'Think how I was brought up! No school; mooning about alone among my father's books; never any chance to pick up all that goes on in schools – throwing balls; ragging; slang; vulgarities; scenes; jealousies!' But would she have become a different, more rounded person if she had experienced all this in company with schoolgirls instead of with her siblings? As for universities, she found academics limp and dull. Visiting Oxford in 1907, when she was twenty-five, she described its atmosphere as 'quite the chilliest and least human known to me. You see brains floating like so many sea-anemones, nor have they shape or colour', and two years later, after another visit, 'There were Regius Professors at dinner, and undergraduates who had won prizes without number and were consequently unable to talk.' In the Oxford chapter of *The Years* she lampooned university life brilliantly. She would have been sucked dry by it. Nor was she denied tuition in her youth. Leslie gave her the run of his extensive library, talked to her about what she read, and encouraged her to write, and on those occasions she felt soothed, stimulated, full of love for this unworldly, distinguished, adorable man. He paid for her to take Greek lessons from Janet Case and Latin from Dr George Warr ('my beloved Warr'). While Vanessa left daily for art college, Virginia remained alone at the top of the house, puzzling over Homer and Sophocles, line by line with a lexicon, naturally studious, and determined to be a writer.

She discovered for herself the pleasure of dipping deep into the treasury of the language to express her exact meaning, partly by writing essays and a diary, but mainly in the form of letters to her family and friends. Often she would write to her brother Thoby at school and later at Cambridge, and he, remarkably for a schoolboy, kept her letters, unlike those which she wrote to me when I was his age. She acquired a gift for self-mockery and the mocking of others, akin to the juvenile burlesques of Jane Austen, for she found disapproval more amusing than approval, but without malice. London, apart from Leslie's tantrums, was fun; so was the country. On holiday in Huntingdonshire in 1899, she wrote to Emma Vaughan: 'I shall think it a test of friends for the future whether they can appreciate the Fen country. I want to read books about it, and to write sonnets about it all day long. It is the only place for rest of mind and body, and for contentment and creamy potatoes and all the joys of life.'

She was honing her gift for observation, and was interested not so much in the weird as in the mysteries of the normal. She scarcely needed formal education. She was her own guide through history and literature. She was learning all through her life.

Another side of her childhood was darker. Her two half-brothers, George and Gerald Duckworth, regarded Vanessa and Virginia as sexual objects, first of wonder, then of desire. Virginia recalled how once at St Ives Gerald lifted her onto a table, and out of curiosity, put his hand under her skirt and examined her private parts. To Virginia, who was always exceptionally modest about her body, this was repulsive. She never forgot it. She did not accuse Gerald of any other indiscretions. George became the monster. After Julia's death, he would enter Virginia's bedroom, fling himself onto her bed, and take her in his arms. She wrote later of his 'violent gusts of passion', and of his behaviour as 'little better than a brute's'. The suggestion was that he had committed, or at least attempted, incest with the girls, and this was Quentin Bell's belief when he first wrote of these incidents. The term 'incestuous relationship' is how he summarized them in the index to the first volume of his Life of his aunt. Other biographers took up the theme. George's behaviour was said to have been responsible for Virginia's sexual timidity and even contributive to her periodic fits of insanity. Louise de Salvo, the American Woolf scholar, has claimed that 'sexual abuse was probably the central and most formative feature of her early life', and she alleges that 'virtually every male member of the Stephen household was engaged in this behaviour'. She uses the term incest without qualification.

The allegation is far-fetched. Soon after Quentin Bell's book was published, I visited George Duckworth's son Henry in his Sussex house to enquire whether his father had kept any letters from Virginia that might throw more light on the matter. Appalled by Bell's innuendoes, he gave me five letters with permission to publish them, because he believed that they would prove beyond doubt that the relationship between George and his half-sisters stopped short of any reasonable reproach. He argued that it was almost inconceivable that a girl who had been subjected to such brutal treatment could address her seducer as 'My dear old Bar' and 'My dearest George', or that Vanessa, the other victim of his endearments, would have gone happily to Paris with him in 1900 and two years later to Rome. Quentin Bell, in his last book, *Elders and Betters*, modified his censure of the Duckworth brothers. He concluded that whatever George's lust may have been, he never carried it to the extent of rape. Nasty erotic fumblings are the most we need suppose. George's instinct was no doubt incestuous, but his practice was not. So conventional a man would never have run the risk of an incestuous and illegitimate child. In recollection, Virginia made more of a drama of the affair than the facts justify.

George's attempt to introduce the sisters to polite London society ended in failure. He himself was handsome and socially ambitious, and no doubt sought to magnify his popularity by association with two exceptionally attractive girls. He assumed the role of their dead mother. To him every party was a challenge to Virginia's and Vanessa's marriageability. He could not understand why they were so ungrateful. He was proud of their beauty: should they not be proud of his? But they refused to act the part he planned for them. 'We are failures really', Virginia wrote to Emma Vaughan. 'We can't shine in society. I don't know how it's done. We ain't popular. We sit in corners and look like mutes who are longing for a funeral.' When they were taken as guests to country houses, it was no better. At Corby Castle, which belonged to Jack Hills's father, 'it was very dismal and strange. Everything is very stately and uncomfortable. I wish to goodness I could find myself at home.' This was written to Thoby.

Then Leslie fell ill with abdominal cancer, and took two years to die. The course of his decline was described by Virginia in almost daily bulletins to her new confidante, Violet Dickinson, who had been Stella's friend, and although she was seventeen years older, Virginia conceived for her an almost passionate affection, writing to her letters that startle us by their frankness: 'It is astonishing what depths – hot volcanic depths – your finger has stirred in Sparroy [her name for herself when writing to Violet], hitherto entirely quiescent.' Their flirtation was carried on step by step with Leslie's decline. Virginia was not heartless, but she could not help revealing to Violet her impatience for his death. On Christmas Day 1903 she wrote, 'If only it could be quicker', but she meant it as much for Leslie's sake as for her own. He died two months later, on 22 February 1904, when Virginia was just twenty-two. She wrote to Janet Case next day, 'Father died very peacefully, as we sat by him. I know it was what he wanted most. All these years we have hardly been apart and I want him every moment of the day. But we still have each other – Nessa and Thoby and Adrian and I, and when we are together, he and Mother do not seem far off.' There was no room for the Duckworths in their little world. Orphaned, they moved as a group, Vanessa taking the lead.

II

A FEW DAYS after Leslie's cremation they went to Manorbier in south Wales, and Violet Dickinson joined them there. It was empty country, between moor and sea, and Virginia walked alone along the cliffs, meditating on her future. In 1922 she recorded in her diary that it was during these walks that the vision of what she wanted to write focussed clearly in her mind, but at the time she made no mention of it in her letters, which dwelt, as so often when a parent dies, on what more she should have done for her father, and her regret that he never knew how much she loved him. Vanessa was harsher. Many years later she confided to her son that Leslie's death had come as a relief. 'It was impossible not to be glad', she said. 'He had been ill for so long, and we had for so long been expecting it, and it was of course in many ways convenient', by which she meant that the four of them could escape from the Duckworths and the stuffy gentility of Hyde Park Gate.

They would find a house for themselves, if possible in Bloomsbury.

Before taking this important step in their lives, the four of them, as if in need of a further purging of the past, went to Italy. It was Virginia's first visit abroad apart from a childhood jaunt to Boulogne, but the holiday was not well managed. Nobody had bothered to book rooms in Venice, and their first gondola trips were in search of lodgings, and when they found them, they were so cramped that they were obliged to move into an expensive hotel which they could ill afford. Only then could Virginia 'wander about open-mouthed', but she was never an avid sightseer, preferring people and pictures to palaces and churches. The party continued to Florence, where they met English friends and were pestered by begging children. Virginia did not think well of the Italians, of whose language she could not speak a word. She thought the country beautiful but its people degenerate. 'Thank God', she wrote to Emma Vaughan, 'that I was born an Englishwoman'. All her life she remained a partial xenophobe.

In Paris, on their way home, they were more fortunate. They found Clive Bell, whom Virginia had met once before in Thoby's rooms at Cambridge, and he took them to visit Auguste Rodin in his studio. Clive was the first non-Duckworth man in Virginia's life, and she loved him for his joviality, intellectual adventurousness and a constant undercurrent of flirtatiousness. She was half amused, half scared, and their friendship would have developed rapidly had she not succumbed, on the day after their return from Paris, to a severe mental breakdown.

'All that summer she was mad', wrote Quentin Bell, and his words were borrowed in 1981 for the title of a book by Dr

Stephen Trombley which set out to prove them unjustified. She was not mad in the technical sense, nor even manic depressive, the looser term often employed by people unqualified to make a judgment. Dr Trombley proposed a more scientific diagnosis: 'She suffered from a complex somatic reaction to a series of difficult personal situations'. But 'mad' was the word employed by Virginia's family and by herself, in faint derision of her condition, because they knew that it would pass, and once passed, her mind would be clarified by it, as a storm clarifies the sky. 'The insane view of life has much to be said for it', she told Emma Vaughan, meaning that imagination is let loose, and some of her best ideas came to her when was in no fit state to record them. But at the time, it was no joke to her family and friends. Once before, following the death of her mother, Virginia had acted very strangely, fainting without reason, blushing when spoken to, and subject to bouts of insomnia and headache, but this second attack, in May–August 1904, was more serious. She refused to eat. She insulted her closest friends. The birds were talking Greek, and Edward VII was yelling obscenities in the shrubbery. Like Septimus Warren Smith in *Mrs Dalloway* she threw herself from a window in attempted suicide, but it failed because the window was too close to the ground. All this time she was staying with Violet Dickinson in Hertfordshire, under the care of three nurses and the eminent nerve specialist George Savage, who had little idea how to treat her dementia or its cause. If this was not madness, it was something akin to it. 'The Goat's mad', her siblings would remark cheerfully, using her childhood nickname. They were not unsympathetic, but busy in arranging the move from Hyde Park Gate to Bloomsbury.

When Virginia recovered, she spent some weeks at Cambridge with her Quaker aunt, Emelia Stephen, who bored her with trivial chatter and tedious benignity, and she busied herself by helping Frederic Maitland with his life of Leslie Stephen, to which she contributed a passage about Leslie as a father. Then, as a further instalment of the convalescence planned for her, she was sent to stay in Yorkshire with her cousin William Vaughan, headmaster of Giggleswick School, and his wife Madge. Life in a headmaster's house was no rest-cure. She was involved in constant meetings with other masters, tea parties with their wives, and compulsory attendance at chapel. She pitied Madge, a woman of stature and literary ambitions, now condemned to intellectual penury. Virginia was well looked after. She was given a large well-windowed bedroom, in which I once spent a night as the guest of a later headmaster, and she could escape from the school to wander on the moors.

Giggleswick also gave her the chance to resume her writing, and for the first time to publish what she wrote. She turned from private journal-keeping to journalism. Violet had introduced her to Mrs Arthur Lyttelton, editor of the Women's Supplement to *The Guardian*, an Anglo-Catholic clerical weekly, and Virginia begged her for work. Her first essay to be published was a description of her visit to Haworth Parsonage, the Brontës' old house. 'There is a knack of writing for newspapers which has to be learnt, and is quite independent of literary merits', she told Violet with the temerity of a first-time journalist. She needed the money after the heavy expenses of her three-month illness, and she invited criticism from her friends, by which she meant praise. Quite soon her gratitude to Margaret Lyttelton changed to indignation that her copy was subjected to minor cuts and alterations. *The Guardian*, which was intended for nuns and clerics, was an absurd medium for a young writer bursting with new ideas. But it was a start. Before long she was invited to contribute reviews to the more prestigious *Times Literary Supplement* and *The National Review*.

Virginia was not the solitary, secretive writer that she later became, hugging her conception to herself like a mother her unborn child. Always relating fact to fancy, she began to define character by body language, clothes and tone of voice, and landscape by the centuries of toil that had created it. Her letters matched her youthful exuberance. When she returned on holiday to Giggleswick, but this time staying in lodgings, liberated from the routines of school life, she wrote to Violet: 'You can imagine that I never wash, or do my hair, but stride with gigantic strides over the wild moorside, shouting Odes of Pindar, as I leap from crag to crag, and exulting in the air which buffets me and caresses me, like a stern but affectionate parent. That is Stephen Brontëised.' Sometimes in writing to Madge Vaughan, who at that period was her literary confidante, she experimented in fumbling terms with a new view of literature, 'a vague and dreamlike world, without love, or heart, or passion, or sex. . . . For though they are dreams to you, and I can't express them at all adequately, these things are perfectly real to me.' She might have been defining *The Waves*.

The Stephen family held together for two years after Leslie's death, years that Virginia described as 'a burst of splendour'. Vanessa organized the move to 46 Gordon Square, Bloomsbury, George Duckworth conveniently married, and his brother Gerald became a publisher, drifting apart from them, so that the Stephens were free to lead their lives untrammelled and unsupervised. They could dress as they wished, eat when and how they wanted, and felt no need to retain friendships imposed on them in their adolescence. Vanessa later wrote, 'It was as if one had stepped suddenly into daylight from darkness'. But their elders saw it as the opposite. Even Henry James was shocked by their disavowal of conventional etiquette. Virginia exulted that at one stroke they abolished the napkin as a symbol of correctness. But there were limits. Vanessa was still addressing Clive, the most intimate of her friends, as 'Dear Mr Bell'.

Bloomsbury itself was symptomatic of their quiet rebelliousness. It was a district of London that in spite of the elegance of its Georgian squares was considered by Kensington to be faintly decadent, the resort of raffish divorcees and indolent students, loose in its morals and behaviour. The Stephens' circumstances matched their income. Leslie Stephen had left property valued at about £15,000, a substantial sum, equivalent to about £350,000 today, and the freehold of Hyde Park Gate, which they chose to lease, not sell, and while neither Thoby nor Adrian earned any money, their sisters were already professionals, Vanessa as a painter (her first paid commission was a portrait of Lady Robert Cecil), and Virginia as a journalist. They could afford to employ two servants, and to take holidays together or separately. Virginia and Adrian went by sea to Portugal and Spain, and all four spent two months in Cornwall and two more in a rented manor house in Norfolk. But it was London that established the pattern of their lives.

First Virginia engaged herself to teach in Morley College in south London, where the poor were offered education after school-age. Her decision was a strange one, possibly inspired by lingering Victorian guilt towards people born without middle-class advantages, or maybe simply from curiosity about other people's lives. For two years she stuck doggedly to this task, teaching English composition, history and literature to classes that could number as few as two students. She was touched by their enthusiasm, but it often waned under pressure, for she started from an utterly different base, and although she tried to simplify her lectures, writing them out beforehand, her audience was apt to dwindle or miss the point. Once, when she had been talking about the Italian Renaissance, the only question was, 'Please, Miss, did the beds in Venice have fleas?'

More important was the slow gathering of like-minded young people at Gordon Square, again on Vanessa's initiative, and the guests, all in their mid-twenties, were mostly Thoby's friends from Cambridge. She formed two weekly soirées, Thursday Evenings and the Friday Club, the latter mainly devoted to the discussion of the arts, but the company on both occasions was interchangeable, apart from Vanessa's girlfriends from the Slade. Among the regular attenders were Lytton Strachey, Clive Bell, Saxon Sydney-Turner, Walter Lamb and Desmond MacCarthy, and a little later, Duncan Grant, Roger Fry and Leonard Woolf, but Leonard for only a single evening before he left to govern part of Ceylon as a colonial civil servant. He was to remain there for seven years.

They were a serious group of young men, and their symposiums in Bloomsbury were at first extensions of their seminars at Cambridge. They read papers to each other and discussed abstract ideas like truth and beauty, fuelled by nothing more than cocoa and a tot of whisky, which was all they could afford. The difference from Cambridge was the presence of the two girls. At the University no girls had been admitted to their society, for although they were known to exist in colleges in the outer suburbs, they were regarded in the same way that monks might regard nuns, unavailable and therefore undesirable. In consequence most of them were homosexual, but not irremediably. Now they were confronted by two young women who not only matched them in intelligence but, as Leonard recalled, were astonishingly beautiful. He later wrote, 'It was almost impossible for a young man not to fall in love with them.' But for the moment, only Clive Bell, the least solemn of the group, dared express his admiration. He proposed to Vanessa, and was refused.

They were dedicated, as Quentin Bell has described, 'to a new honesty and a new charity in personal relations', but one must not imagine that their conversation was always scintillating. Virginia was often in despair at her failure to strike a spark. Though at that stage of her life she was both eager and reserved, like Rachel Vinrace in *The Voyage Out*, she did not take immediately to Thoby's friends. Duncan Grant remembered that she was a little aloof, never addressing the company at large, only individuals. Even that could be tough going. When Sydney-Turner and Strachey joined them for a few days in Cornwall in September 1905, she wrote to Violet: 'They are a great trial. They sit silent, absolutely silent, all the time; occasionally they escape to a corner and chuckle over a Latin joke. Perhaps they are falling in love with Nessa; who knows? It would be a silent and very learned process. However, I don't think they are robust enough to feel very much. Oh, women are my line, and not these inanimate creatures.' She was exaggerating. If these parties were truly so melancholy, she would not have repeated them year after year. These 'inanimate creatures' were to become her most intimate friends and shared with her the 'burst of splendour' that followed her escape from Kensington. But apart from Clive they seemed to lack her vitality. There was no Byron or Trelawny among them. They were embarrassed by their friend's sisters. It was not until they came to discard their Cambridge asceticism that their company was enjoyable. Even Leonard struck Virginia at their first meeting as 'a violent, trembling, misanthropic Jew'. She remained devoted to her few women friends, and only once did she consent to attend a party in the smart world that she had renounced. 'I went to a dance last night', she told Violet, 'and found a dim corner where I sat and read *In Memoriam*, while Nessa danced every dance till 2.30.' Vanessa, who was to become the more exclusive and reclusive of the sisters, was now the more audacious. 'She has volcanoes under her sedate manner', Virginia wrote about her, and to her, 'You are the most complete human being of us all.'

In September 1906 the quartet went to Greece, and then onwards to Turkey. It was the only holiday that Virginia took outside Europe, and had it not been that illness spoiled its last stages, it was for her an unforgettable experience. Drenched in classical history and literature (she carried the *Odyssey* in her handbag), her only regret was that the 5th century BC was succeeded by civilizations that could not match it for originality and zest, and she cared little for their monuments.

She and Vanessa, with Violet Dickinson, travelled by train through France and Italy, and by sea from Brindisi to Patras, from where it was but a short step to the classic site of Olympia. There they were joined by Thoby and Adrian, who had sailed down the Dalmatian coast and took horse through Montenegro. Their reunion was followed by visits to Corinth and Nauplia. At Mycenae they stayed in the inn named after Helen of Troy, where thirty years later I found their signatures in the visitors' book. Virginia kept a careful journal of their travels, which was edited in 1990 by Mitchell Leaska. Her description of Mycenae contains the sentence, 'I conceived that here was a single spot of intense and brilliantly painted life, girt in by great wastes of desert land'. She was never a guidebook addict: she wrote her own. As Leaska commented, 'Something new and different was finding its way into her style. ... Her imagery was becoming more impressionistic, ambiguous, and therefore more resonant, in sound and meaning', a quality that was to distinguish all her writing.

At Athens Vanessa fell ill, and was cared for by Violet while the others visited friends in Euboea. She recovered sufficiently to continue to Constantinople with all of them except Thoby, who returned to London. Virginia was impressed by the Turks. Religion was a natural part of their daily life: they could turn to their devotions as easily as to their ledgers. Many of the women walked without covering their faces, and she wondered why it had ever been necessary to hide the face 'of a benevolent spinster, with gold rims to her spectacles, trotting out to buy a fowl for dinner. What danger has she got to hide from?'

Vanessa was still unwell, and they thought it would be wiser to cut short their holiday and travel home by the Orient Express. At Dover, Violet, too, was taken ill, and they were met by the news that Thoby was in bed with a high fever. They had succumbed to what was at first assumed by the doctors to be malaria, but was then diagnosed as acute typhoid. Thoby and Violet lay scarcely a mile apart, desperately ill. She recovered, but Thoby died on 20 November 1906, aged twenty-six.

His death was shocking to his friends. He was in the prime of life, handsome, attractive, vivacious. He was Virginia's idolized brother. She had loved him as a schoolboy, worshipped him as an undergraduate. Adrian was no substitute. His daughter later admitted, 'The wrong brother died', and though Virginia and Vanessa never said this, they felt it. Adrian was a good, clever, affectionate man, but Virginia still thought of him as a 'poor little boy' when he was aged twenty-three and 6 ft. 5 in. tall. She felt Thoby's death so acutely that she concealed it for nearly a month from Violet, even inventing bulletins of his recovery long after he had died, in case the shock should kill her too. She reserved the expression of her grief for *Jacob's Room*, where Jacob is a recognizable portrait of Thoby, and his journey through Greece was almost mile by mile the one they had taken together.

Then, in scarcely less dramatic circumstances, Virginia lost her sister too. Two days after Thoby's death ('indecently soon', Virginia felt), Clive Bell proposed to Vanessa a second time, and she accepted him. He was Thoby's closest friend, in some ways his *alter ego*, but Vanessa was not in love with him, merely grateful for his kindness to her during Thoby's illness, and happy that he loved art and possessed the gift of making other people happy. Both were highly sensual. I remember a discussion at a men's dining club about the most important discoveries of the twentieth century. Some people nominated the telephone, the aeroplane, the radio. 'What do you think, Clive?', one of us asked. 'The most important discovery of the century', he replied, 'is that women like it too.'

Clive took his fiancée – the word seemed ludicrous to them, but there was no other – to meet his parents in their house in Wiltshire, and foolishly invited Virginia to join them. While Vanessa was obliged to express some pleasure in the visit, Virginia was under no such obligation, and all her contempt for middle-class respectability spilled into her letter to Violet Dickinson: 'The thickness of this nib and the luxury of this paper will show you that I am in a rich and illiterate house, set in its own grounds, gothic, barbaric. I dip my pen into the hoof of an old hunter.' Clive's mother was a 'little rabbit-faced woman, with wisps of white hair', his father 'an obvious country gentleman', and their daughters 'exactly what one would have guessed. They play hockey and beagle, and laugh at Adrian's jokes and come down to dinner in pale blue satin with satin bows in their hair.' She found it difficult to believe that Clive had remained unaffected by this background. She pitied her sister.

This was a very temporary phase of jealousy, for soon after Vanessa's marriage in February 1907, Virginia found in Clive a correspondent in whom she could confide and a friend who shared her dislike of domesticity which the birth of her son Julian forced on Vanessa. Virginia could tolerate children for short periods, but fled from babies. 'I doubt that I shall ever have a baby', she wrote to Violet from Cornwall, where she, the baby and its parents were on holiday. 'Its voice is too terrible, a senseless scream like an ill-omened cat. Nobody could pretend that it was a human being.' Clive refused to cuddle it. It leaked unpleasantly from every orifice. So Clive and Virginia were thrown together by this infant, and they found in each other an escape. Quentin Bell, Vanessa's second son, has called it more than a flirtation. He claimed that

Virginia's motive was 'to break down that charmed circle within which Vanessa and Clive were so happy, and by which she was so cruelly excluded'. Her behaviour, like Clive's, was inexcusable. She set out to detach her sister from him, while he by his response to her showed how shallow was his love for Vanessa. Frances Spalding, Vanessa's biographer, has summed up the affair (Virginia's own term for it) as 'more a game of wits than a matter of passion, but this did not lessen the outrage'. Virginia soon came to regret her treachery, and for the rest of her life treated her sister with loving caution, to which Vanessa, the stronger character of the two, did not always respond. Clive, on the other hand, showed no symptom of remorse, and his relations with Virginia were undamaged. She found him the most sympathetic and intelligent of all those whom she consulted on the topic that meant most to her, her writing. Indeed he was the only person to whom she ever showed a book in draft, her first, *Melymbrosia*, which she began to write in 1907 and published eight years later under the title *The Voyage Out*.

The original Hyde Park Gate family of ten was now reduced to two, Virginia and Adrian. Julia, Stella, Leslie and Thoby were dead, George and Vanessa married, Gerald a publisher, Laura locked up mad. As it was clearly impossible for Virginia and Adrian to share Gordon Square with their married sister, they searched Bloomsbury for another house, and eventually found 29 Fitzroy Square, only a few blocks away, thus initiating those moves from square to square that continued throughout the next three decades, like a game of chess, but never overstepping the boundaries of the board that was Bloomsbury.

Having established themselves so agreeably, Virginia and

her brother were continually travelling. Fundamentally she was an urban woman: she needed the society of friends, and ready access to libraries, picture galleries, theatres and concert halls. But she was rural too. She loved long and solitary country walks, and although she had no knowledge of horticulture, agriculture or wild animals, she enjoyed the queer shapes and sounds of the countryside, the flight of birds and a fox's bark. Thus we find her and Adrian spending the Christmas of 1906 in a cottage in the New Forest, the following summer in a rented house at Rye in Sussex, and in 1908 she took lodgings by herself at Wells in Somerset and revisited Manorbier in Wales.

She kept in touch by letter-writing. Even after the telephone became easily available, the letter was her medium. She would write several on most days, of which about a fifth have survived, and I, who edited them in six volumes with Joanne Trautmann, have been rereading them with renewed astonishment at their versatility. She might write three long letters to different correspondents in an evening without repeating a single phrase from one into another. They vary in depth and speed, like a stream now running fast over pebbles, now settling into pools. Their mood is almost invariably cheerful, merry, solicitous. When she gossiped (which was frequently) it was not with malice, but as a caricature. Take, for example, her famous description of her meeting with Henry James in Rye:

> He fixed me with his staring blank eye – it is like a child's marble – and said, 'My dear Virginia, they tell me – they tell me – they tell me – that you – as indeed being your father's daughter nay your grandfather's grandchild – the descendant I may say of a

century – of a century – of quill pens and ink – ink – ink pots, yes, yes, yes, they tell me – ahm m m – that you, that you, that you *write* in short.' This went on in the public street, while we all waited, as farmers wait for a hen to lay an egg – do they? – nervous, polite, and now on this foot now on that. I felt like a condemned person, who sees the knife drop and stick and drop again.

Virginia was not then the alarming person that she became, unintentionally but inevitably, when she was famous. Meeting her for the first time you might have considered her timid, shy. Such an encounter was recorded by Arnold Bennett when he met her in a Paris café in April 1907: 'Young Bell [Clive] was there with his wife, who is a daughter of Leslie Stephen. Another daughter [Virginia] and a son [Adrian] came in. Bell's wife was slightly attractive; the other daughter not – I mean physically. All seemed very decent, quiet young people, carrying very well the weight of their name', when that was the very weight that they had succeeded in shaking off. As for their appearance, Bennett's judgment is contradicted by every contemporary compliment and photograph. He was expecting two pretty girls. He met two sophisticated young women.

Two men fell seriously in love with Virginia. One was Walter Headlam, a lecturer in classics at King's College, Cambridge, whom she liked well enough to lend him her manuscripts for criticism, but he was old enough to be her father and died quite suddenly in 1908. The other was Hilton Young, the assistant editor of *The Economist* and an habitué of Thursday Evenings. Virginia played him like a fish, dangling herself like a bait before him, and then withdrawing. Eventually he proposed to her, and she refused him, saying that she could marry nobody but Lytton Strachey. But when Lytton did propose to her in February 1909, she changed her mind twenty-four hours after accepting him, to the evident relief of both of them. 'He's perfect as a friend', she told Molly MacCarthy, 'but he's a female friend.'

III

IN SPITE OF these distractions, the ten years before the outbreak of war marked the full flowering of Bloomsbury. In 1982 I lectured about this celebrated group of friends at Austin, Texas, and warned my academic audience that there was a danger that in America they might be overestimating, and we in Britain underestimating, their influence and achievement. Our Virginia, I said, had become their Woolf, and they were not the same person. While for American scholars Bloomsbury still bulks large in the development of twentieth-century ideas on feminism, socialism and pacifism, the British are more cautious, less exclamatory, sometimes downright hostile, looking for the pioneers of these movements more to the Fabians, the Webbs, Wells, Shaw, Marie Stopes, Ethel Smyth, Emmeline Pankhurst and Millicent Fawcett, who were contemporaries of the Bloomsbury group but by no possible definition members of it. Americans, I said, may inadvertently be moulding the Bloomsberries into their preconceived notions of them, and putting into their mouths things that they wish they had said and meant, but didn't actually say or mean, while we may be dismissing important things that they did say as plagiarisms or platitudes.

If it can be said that a Group exists and has an identity, it must hold certain ideas in common and a wish to propagate them. In Bloomsbury I find it hard to define what those ideas were, beyond claiming in the loosest sense that they were more liberated than their predecessors, expressed themselves more frankly, treated women as equals to men and had a respect for intellectual excellence. But that does not amount to a doctrine. Michael Holroyd has pointed out that it is quite untrue that they shared a philosophy or a system of aesthetics, and those who claim that they did, 'understand next to nothing of the isolated way in which a work of art is evolved'. Forster's novels owed nothing to Virginia's, Strachey's theory of civilization little to Clive Bell's. Or take Leonard Woolf's thinking on international relations, and Keynes's on economics: in no way could it be said that it was a Bloomsbury way of thinking. There was a little more community of taste in art and music, and negatively they were linked by their indifference to science and religion, as well as by their pacifism in the First World War. Their socialism was tepid: it assumed the perpetuity of the capitalist system and the subordination of the servant class. Virginia's championship of women's rights did not extend far down the social scale. She never protested that it was the lot of most women to remain at home and cook their husbands' dinners. She was anxious that more women of her own class should have the opportunity to become doctors, lawyers, teachers, writers, but she felt no need to argue that secretaries should become directors of their companies if they were clever enough, or that cleaning ladies might by their own efforts rise to become ladies for whom other ladies cleaned.

That is the negative side. More positively it should be emphasized that this small group of men and women exerted in several directions a beneficent influence of which we are the inheritors. Each in his or her own way was attempting the most difficult feat that a man or woman can undertake – to give an art or a doctrine a new shape which survives challenge and ridicule to be accepted as non-controversial decades later. Virginia Woolf and E.M. Forster achieved this by their novels; Duncan Grant, Vanessa Bell and Roger Fry by their own paintings and advocacy of the French. Lytton Strachey revolutionized biography; T.S. Eliot, poetry; Desmond MacCarthy, literary criticism; Leonard Woolf, international affairs (he wrote the first draft of the Charter of the League of Nations); Keynes, economics. And all of them by their conduct can teach us how to live, how to allocate our time, how to be happy, how to love.

The fascination that these people still exert is partly due to the vast amount of information we have about them. The discovery of their intimacies, the cat's cradle of their cor-respondence, generates a vicarious excitement in all who study their works and days. We are privileged to know more about them than any of them knew about the others. They were the first to regard homosexuality as normal: it was a joyful consequence of friendship. If they were unfaithful to each other, their infidelities tended to be permanent and only temporarily resented. Bloomsbury's greatest legacy, indeed, was their concept of friendship. Nothing – not age, nor success, nor rivalry in art or love, nor different careers and branching intimacies, nor separation for long periods by war, travel or occupation – ever parted these people who first came together when they were young.

There is no doubt that their society was exclusive and alarming. I can just remember what it was like, because once, when I was aged about twelve, I was taken by my mother to a Bloomsbury party. The room was large, smoky and warmed more by excitement than by artificial means. There were divans and carpets, walls painted gaudily like a seraglio, gramophone records on trays and books everywhere. People were sitting on the floor at other people's feet, and there was much noise and laughter, high-pitched and faintly neighing, which ceased suddenly on the arrival of people like us. My mother and I found a corner where we could sit more or less unobserved, and I was given a tomato sandwich. People were jumping up all the time, reaching for a book, peering at a picture. There was an undercurrent of competitiveness, as if everyone had to justify their presence each time afresh. On one such occasion, when Virginia had told one of her funniest stories and the laughter had died down, she turned to a girl of eighteen and said, 'Now you tell us a story'. Of course it wasn't kind. It was not intended to be. Bloomsbury demanded that you catch the ball when it was thrown in your direction and if you missed it, you were not invited again, and didn't wish to be.

In his diary, quoted by his nephew Quentin in his biography of Virginia, Adrian Stephen recorded an incident that must have been typical. It was at an impromptu party in July 1909 at Fitzroy Square. People slowly drifted in, uninvited:

Saxon Sydney-Turner, Lytton Strachey and his brother James came first; then Clive, Vanessa, Duncan Grant and Henry Lamb.

'The conversation', wrote Adrian, 'kept up a good flow, though it was not very interesting, until at about half-past eleven Miss Cole arrived. She went and sat in the long wicker chair with Virginia and Clive on the floor beside her. Virginia began in her usual tone of frank admiration to compliment her on her appearance: "Of course you, Miss Cole, are always dressed so exquisitely. You look so original, so like a seashell. There is something so refined about you coming in among our muddy boots and pipe smoke, dressed in your exquisite creations". Clive chimed in with more heavy compliments, and then began asking her why she disliked him so much, saying how any other young lady would have been much pleased with all the nice things he had been saying, but she treated him so sharply. At this Virginia interrupted with, "I think Miss Cole has a very strong character", and so on. . . . The poor woman was the centre of all our gaze, and did not know what to do with herself.'

Now, Annie Cole was no mouse. Two years later she married Neville Chamberlain, and when he became Prime Minister, she took on an important part in international politics.

Virginia's conduct on this occasion was her mordant side. When friends fell ill, or were bereaved, or long absent abroad, or crossed in love, she could show great sympathy. But she never hesitated to lampoon them, put them at jumps which she knew they could not clear, and invent for them situations ('I know what you have been doing this morning: you have been riding a white horse down Piccadilly') which exposed them to ridicule. Her chaff was not confined to outsiders like Miss Cole. Members of Bloomsbury were ruthless in criticism of each other's books, pictures and attitudes. The most false of all legends about them is that they were a mutual admiration society. On the contrary, they set themselves standards of integrity and originality so high that they constantly fell short of them, and they said so, without malice, in speech or a flurry of letters. Sometimes their mock insults were direct. Virginia could write to Violet Dickinson, 'Adrian thinks he met you today. The lady smiled – was it you or a prostitute?', and Violet was supposed not to mind. They were so keen to amuse each other that they exaggerated their friends' failings and misfortunes, magnified their own small adventures, and gilded every lily richly. It was an abrasive society, highly stimulating. It was said that the difference between Blooms-bury and Cambridge was that at Cambridge nothing witty was said unless it was also profound, and in Bloomsbury nothing profound was said unless it was also witty. Virginia was largely responsible for this change in mood.

In August 1909 she went with Adrian and Saxon Sydney-Turner to Bayreuth and Dresden, and relieved her boredom by writing acerbic letters to Vanessa. *Parsifal* was a tedious opera, she thought, 'weak and vague stuff', and Saxon 'rather peevish. He hops along humming like a stridulous grass-hopper. He clenches his fists, scowls, and stops at once if you look at him.' As for the natives, her xenophobia surfaced again: 'I haven't seen one German woman who has a face; they are puddings of red dough.'

In 1910 Virginia made two political gestures. She was per-suaded by Janet Case to join the Women's Suffrage Move-ment, and while she could in no way be described as a militant, she spent hours in the movement's offices addressing envelopes to indifferent politicians. The campaign had been gaining popular support for years, but the Prime Minister, Asquith, was a strong opponent, and his refusal to grant the vote to women led to increasing protests and violence. The outbreak of war in 1914 halted the campaign but gained its object. Most women were granted the vote in 1918. Virginia took no further part in the movement, regarding political agitation as foolish, even when she sympathized with its causes and benefited from its results.

It is therefore all the more surprising that she allowed herself to be drawn into the Dreadnought Hoax in February 1910. The details have been well recorded by Adrian and Virginia herself, and amplified by their biographers. It was the event that first drew attention to Bloomsbury. Their success in hoodwinking the Royal Navy shocked and amused the public, but few people realized that the hoax was not just the prank of a few mischievous young men and women, but a political and pacifist statement.

The plan was the joint concept of Adrian and his friend Horace Cole (a brother of Annie), who was renowned for his practical jokes. They proposed to expose the Navy to ridicule by staging a formal visit by 'the Emperor of Abyssinia' to the fleet's newest and most prestigious battleship, the *Dreadnought*, then moored in Weymouth harbour. They sent a telegram to the commander-in-chief, purporting to come from the Foreign Office, instructing him to receive the Emperor and his suite with honour. The conspirators then hired a theatrical costumier to dress them appropriately, Adrian as the British interpreter and Cole as the Foreign Office official. All the others blackened their faces and wore heavy disguise. Duncan and Virginia were both in robes, turbans and false moustaches. They had themselves photographed, and set off by train for Weymouth, practising *en route* a fictional language that they hoped would be taken for something faintly aboriginal.

There are two unexplained puzzles. Why did Virginia consent to take part in this escapade? She was not by nature a practical joker. She had no acting ability. She hardly knew Cole, and Adrian had little influence on her. Vanessa strongly discouraged her. At that stage of her life she had given little thought to the iniquities of armies and navies. But she never regretted taking part, and as late as 1940 lectured on the hoax with amusement and a certain pride. It was a successful lark, and in later life she attributed to it a moral motive that can scarcely have occurred to her at the time.

The second puzzle is why the Navy was taken in. The authenticity of the Foreign Office telegram was never checked, the disguises never penetrated. The party were given a red-carpet welcome at Weymouth, and conducted by launch to the *Dreadnought*, where the Admiral received them on the quarterdeck with his flag-Commander, William Fisher, Virginia's cousin (who might well have recognized her and Adrian), and they were shown round the most modern and secret of Britain's warships. They were offered refreshments, which they declined on religious grounds, but in reality for fear that their makeup might run, and a twenty-one-gun salute, which they generously declared to be unnecessary. Then they returned to London.

Cole, delighted with the success of the hoax, leaked the story to the newspapers. Indeed, there would have been no purpose in it unless it was to become public knowledge.

Questions were asked in Parliament, but the fuss was minimal compared to what it would have been today. The most severe punishment suffered by the conspirators was a ceremonial tap on Cole's and Duncan's bottoms, inflicted by young officers to restore the Navy's honour. Cole consented to this chastisement on condition that he could tap them back. The only older people to be outraged by the incident were members of the Stephen family and the Fishers.

This incident was in no way responsible for Virginia's mental breakdown later in that year. She suffered from headaches and insomnia, and seemed once again on the verge of insanity. Visits to Cornwall, Dorset and a rented house near Canterbury failed to restore her. In late June 1910 Dr Savage advised her to enter a mental nursing home for six weeks, but her condition was not serious enough to prevent her mocking it in letters to Vanessa and her friends. She showed great fortitude, shut up with mad women in a hideous house, while she herself was not mad enough to be unaware of their madness. 'I feel my brains, like a pear', she wrote from her prison, 'to see if it's ripe: it will be exquisite by September.'

After a convalescence in Cornwall and Dorset, it was. She was able to resume work on *Melymbrosia*, her novel, and give a little time to Women's Suffrage. But the main excitement of the autumn, and Bloomsbury's major pre-war claim to fame, was the First Post-Impressionist Exhibition. The guiding inspiration was Roger Fry's. The Bells had first met him early in the year, and he was captivated by Bloomsbury, as Bloomsbury was by him. He determined to confront English society with the paintings and sculpture of modern French artists, whose very names – Cézanne, Van Gogh, Matisse, Picasso – were almost unknown in Britain, and with

Desmond MacCarthy as his adjutant, he ransacked the studios and galleries of Paris to bring back examples of their work and present them to the public in the Grafton Galleries. The exhibition caused a sensation. The pictures were reviled even by innovative British painters like Walter Sickert. They were called 'pornographic', 'the work of madmen'. Laughter mingled with pretended revulsion.

Virginia had little to do with mounting the exhibition, and supported it hesitantly from the sidelines, but it affected her strongly. What the artists were doing in paint (disdaining what Vanessa called the 'fatal prettiness' of conventional British art), she intended to pioneer in prose, giving the essence of a person or a place without describing it precisely. As Desmond MacCarthy put it in his Introduction to the catalogue, 'A good rocking horse has often more of the true horse about it than an instantaneous photograph of a Derby winner'. 'Art', said Fry, 'is significant deformity.' For example, Duncan Grant's portrait of Virginia painted at this time, and now in the Metropolitan Museum, New York, is unrecognizable as her – it might be a fishwife – but it reflects Virginia's brooding contemplation, while in Vanessa's portrait of her, painted in the next year, her left eye is entirely missing. Virginia made no protest. It was a breaking of convention. The fashionable world did not see it like this. The suffragettes, the Dreadnought Hoax, and now this exhibition, were all part of a deplorable attack on taste and good manners. When Virginia and Vanessa appeared at the Post-Impressionist Ball dressed in gaudy draperies and very little underneath, it was taken as further proof that the younger generation were inebriated by a passing French fashion.

In April 1911 Vanessa, Clive, Roger Fry and Harry Norton

went to Turkey on holiday, and while there, Vanessa fell seriously ill after a miscarriage. Virginia, intensely worried by rumours of her condition, hastened to join them – it was her second visit to Turkey – and brought her sister back by train. Her help was scarcely needed. Fry, not Clive, took control. He was solicitous and amazingly competent. In the process, he fell in love with Vanessa, and she with him. From that moment the Bell marriage was transformed into what her son Quentin has called a 'union of friendship'.

Virginia had no lover and no wish for one, and turned down two further offers of marriage, one from Walter Lamb (Henry's brother), the other from the diplomatist, Sydney Waterlow, who was divorcing his wife in the hope of marrying her. In writing to Sydney, Virginia was kind ('I don't think I shall ever feel for you what I must feel for the man I marry'), but in writing about him, she did not spare him her sharpest ridicule. She needed solitude to complete her book, and bought one half of a Victorian house at Firle, her first venture into the part of east Sussex which was to be her country retreat for the rest of her life. She agreed that 'the cottage' was in fact 'a hideous suburban villa', the only ugly house in a pretty village, but that didn't matter, because when you are inside, you can forget the outside. It was also a good base for walking on the Downs. Here she remained for much of the summer of 1911, revising her novel, and broke off only to stay with Ottoline Morrell, and go camping in Devon with Rupert Brooke, his lover Ka Cox, and Maynard Keynes.

Virginia painted in 1911–12 by her sister Vanessa Bell, a portrait now in the National Portrait Gallery. The portrait soon followed the Post-Impressionist Exhibition, which strongly influenced Vanessa's art, and indirectly Virginia's writing. 'Her left eye is entirely missing, but she made no protest.'

IV

LEONARD WOOLF RETURNED on leave from Ceylon determined to marry Virginia. Although they had not once corresponded during his seven-year absence, he was encouraged by Lytton Strachey's letters to think that she might accept him. They met several times after his return, and she was happy to notice that he was unchanged by 'shooting tigers, hanging natives and ruling a province the size of Wales', as she chose to imagine his life of exile, and he slipped back easily into Bloomsbury moods and manners. He did not have the wit of Lytton Strachey, the sparkle of Roger Fry nor the geniality of Clive Bell, but he had an exceptionally fertile and original mind, and Virginia already loved him because he had loved Thoby. The only permanent mark left on his character by his colonial career, as he admitted in his autobiography, was, 'I was a stickler for what was officially right and proper'. I remember him as kind but rather formidable. His awkwardness with children made us awkward too. His hands trembled all the time. He could not lift a cup of tea without spilling it. That fascinated us. In her diary, twenty-five years later, Virginia speculated that this trembling, which had persisted since infancy, may have 'moulded his life wrongly. All his shyness, his suffering from society, his sharpness and definiteness, might have been smoothed' had it not been for this affliction. To think of this gaunt man in his ill-fitting suit as an ardent lover strains the imagination, but he was.

Virginia invited him to stay several times at Firle, and on

one of their walks over the Downs they discovered Asheham, a pretty Regency house, of which Virginia took a joint lease with Vanessa, and they moved there from Firle at the end of 1911. At about the same time, the lease of Fitzroy Square ran out, and she rented 38 Brunswick Square, a large Bloomsbury house which she shared with Adrian, Maynard Keynes and Duncan Grant. In December they were joined there by Leonard Woolf. It was the first of their houses to be equipped with a telephone, and Virginia accepted the device without excitement, still relying on letters as the civilized way for friends to communicate when apart. In consequence we can know a great deal about the progress of Leonard's courtship.

The intimacy between them grew fast. He first proposed to her in January 1912, and she gently repulsed him. She hesitated again in May when he renewed his appeal, and gave him her reasons candidly. Her mind was unstable, she said: she might become a burden to him. Then, 'I feel angry sometimes at the strength of your desire', which she might be unable to reciprocate. Next, 'possibly your being a Jew comes in also at this point'. This was not too serious an objection, but Virginia had inherited a certain anti-Semitic prejudice from her father. Her letters are speckled with evidence of it. 'There are a great many Portuguese Jews on board and other repulsive objects', she had written to Violet Dickinson in 1905 when she was on her way to Spain. She wrote again to her in 1910, 'I sat on a platform next to Portuguese Jews, whose sweat ran into powder, caked and blew off.' As late as 1933, she described the eminent philosopher, Isaiah Berlin, on first meeting him, as 'a Portuguese Jew, by the look of him' (why always Portuguese?). She came to boast of Leonard's Jewishness as if it was to her credit that she married him in spite of it. In 1930 she told Ethel Smyth, 'How I hated marrying a Jew – how I hated their nasal voices, and their oriental jewellery, and their noses and their wattles – what a snob I was, for they have immense vitality.' She was not alone in thinking this. In *The Years* (1937) one hears the voice of her class and generation:

'Was someone coming in?' Her eyes were on the door.

'The Jew', she murmured.

'The Jew', he said.

They listened. He could hear quite distinctly now. Somebody was turning on taps; somebody was having a bath in the room opposite.

'The Jew having a bath', she said.

'The Jew having a bath', he repeated.

'And tomorrow there'll be a line of grease round the bath', she said.

'Damn the Jew!', he exclaimed.

Hermione Lee has pointed out in her biography of Virginia Woolf that anti-Semitism in upper-class England persisted well into the inter-war period. We must not make too much of it in Virginia's case, because she didn't; but it was unpleasant.

Leonard sensed that her reservations about marrying him amounted to consent. Vanessa encouraged him ('You are the only person I know whom I can imagine as her husband'), and Virginia showed no resentment of his eagerness. So he took the risk of resigning from the Colonial Service, and waited. Then, quite suddenly, on 29 May, after they had been lunching together in Brunswick Square, she told him that she loved him and would marry him. They went rowing on the

Leonard Woolf by Vanessa Bell. 'To think of this gaunt man in his ill-fitting suit as an ardent lover strains the imagination, but he was.'

Thames to calm down. She broke the news to all her friends (to Janet Case she wrote, 'I am going to marry Leonard Wolf [sic] – he is a penniless Jew'), and was introduced by Leonard to his mother at her house in Putney. It was not a success. Mrs Woolf, to her understandable distress, was not invited to her son's wedding. It took place on 10 August 1912 at St Pancras Registry Office in London, in the presence of Vanessa, the Duckworth brothers, Duncan Grant, Roger Fry and one or two others. Clive gave them lunch in Gordon Square. So they were married. Virginia was thirty, Leonard thirty-one.

If a honeymoon is the first test of a couple's compatibility, it can be said that in all but one sense theirs was a success. After one night at Asheham, they spent nearly a week in the Plough Inn at Holford in Somerset, where their love-making must have been disturbed by the rowdiness at the bar below that continues to this day, and then they went for six weeks to France, Spain and Italy, recording their adventures in letters that lost nothing in frankness. Bloomsbury was agog to know how the wife, as virginal as her name, had coped with her husband's legitimate desire. She did not cope well. From Saragossa she wrote to Ka Cox, 'Why do you think that people make such a fuss about marriage and copulation? I certainly find the climax immensely exaggerated.' Leonard confessed to Vanessa that Virginia's performance, from his point of view, had been most unsatisfactory. Vanessa suggested that he might try a whip. However, this was not the end of their sexual experiments. For several more months they shared a bed, for several years a bedroom, and it was not until Leonard was advised by her doctors that Virginia was too delicate in mind and body to bear a child, and that sexual excitement might trigger off a new attack of madness, that they decided to give up. Thereafter, though they almost always slept under the same roof, it was rarely under the same ceiling. But they continued to kiss and cuddle. Once I applied the word 'frigid' to Virginia's sexuality. It was mistaken. Her letters to Leonard, and his to her, on the rare occasions when they were apart, are full of ardour. In April 1916, for example, she wrote to him, 'There's no doubt that I'm terribly in love with you. I keep thinking what you're doing, and have to stop – it makes me want to kiss you so.' Their correspondence makes it almost certain that for the thirty years of their marriage, Leonard remained in effect chaste, sublimating by his work the passionate love that Virginia denied him.

If their honeymoon had failed to conceive a child, they returned with the literary equivalent – the revised manuscripts of twin novels, one by each of them. Leonard's was *The Village in the Jungle*, based on his experiences in Ceylon; Virginia's was *Melymbrosia*, now renamed *The Voyage Out*, on which she had been working for the same seven years that Leonard had been abroad. His book was published soon after their return. Virginia's was further delayed by her dissatisfaction with it (after five drafts!), and it was only in March 1913 that she delivered the typescript to the only publisher she knew, her half-brother, Gerald Duckworth. For a month she anxiously awaited the verdict of a man whom she despised. Gerald accepted it, but again there was a long delay due to Virginia's recurring illnesses. *The Voyage Out* was not published until March 1915, by which time she was once again insane.

It was mainly the strain of finishing and revising the book, 'with a kind of tortured intensity' as Leonard observed, that caused her breakdown, but there were other stresses too – the punishing schedules that they imposed on themselves, and in August 1914, the outbreak of war. At first they divided their time between lodgings in London's legal district and Asheham. Leonard began to involve himself deeply in politics and journalism, specially in connection with the Cooperative Movement in the Midlands and the north as far as Glasgow, where Virginia accompanied him, bemused by people and causes quite alien to Bloomsbury, but she remained complacent out of loyalty to Leonard. They were obliged to earn money. One cannot claim that they were desperately poor. Virginia had inherited her share of her father's, Stella's, Thoby's and Aunt Emelia's legacies, about £9,000, which, when invested, gave them an income of £400. Leonard had no fixed job, and capital of only £500, the balance of the £690 he had won in a sweepstake. It was not enough. What with the expense of two houses, travel between them, servants in each place, entertainment and books, they needed an income double what their capital could provide. They could not live by novel-writing. In fifteen years *The Voyage Out* earned Virginia less than £120. So Leonard worked doggedly as a political journalist, and she resumed her articles and reviews for the *Times Literary Supplement* until the strain became too great for her, and she collapsed.

Her strong intellect matched her soaring imagination, and her imagination sometimes took control. She talked wildly, suffered from acute headaches, heard strange voices, and could not sleep and would not eat. For three months in 1913 her condition deteriorated to such an extent that there was talk of certifying her insane, and Leonard thought it wise to send her back to the nursing-home in Twickenham where she had been two years earlier. She made hardly any protest, writing to him touchingly affectionate letters ('I got up and dressed last night after you were gone, wanting to come back to you. You do represent all that's best, and I lie here thinking of you'). After two weeks under care, she was well enough to return to Asheham, but there her mind deteriorated once more. On the doctor's strange advice, Leonard took her to the very inn at Holford where they had spent part of their honeymoon. It did no good. She was still hearing voices. So they returned to London, staying with Adrian in Brunswick Square, and there, for the second time in her life, Virginia attempted suicide. Leonard had left unlocked a phial of veronal tablets which he had given her from time to time to help her sleep. While he was out of the house, she swallowed a hundred of them, and sank immediately into a coma. Fortunately, Geoffrey Keynes, Maynard's brother and a surgeon at St Bartholomew's Hospital, who was sharing Adrian's rooms, realized at once that she was on the point of death, and drove her at speed through the streets, shouting at the police, 'Doctor, doctor! Urgent, urgent!', and managed to reach the hospital in time to apply a stomach pump which saved her life. It was two days before she recovered consciousness.

Asheham was not large enough to accommodate the nurses she now needed, and they accepted the offer of her half-brother, George Duckworth, to loan them his Sussex mansion, Dalingridge Hall, complete with servants and every luxury. There they stayed for two months. In the summer of 1914 they moved back to Asheham, and were there when war broke out in August. They saw no reason to cancel a holiday they had planned in Northumberland, and on their return looked for new lodgings. After spending two months on The

Green in Richmond, one of the loveliest parts of London before parked cars destroyed its serenity, they found an idyllic place with a hundred-foot garden, Hogarth House, also in Richmond, which they managed to rent. How their straitened finances and their battered furniture stood up to these constant moves is unexplained.

It was while Leonard was negotiating the lease of Hogarth House in February 1915 that Virginia suffered yet another mental breakdown, her worst. Leonard described her condition as 'a nightmare world of frenzy, despair and violence'. It was not, as previously, simply a matter of insomnia and refusal to eat. She had crossed the borderline between a mental illness of which she was fully conscious to a state of garrulous insanity, speaking incoherently and without pause, sometimes for hours on end until she lost consciousness. Leonard could do nothing for her. She would seldom speak to him except to abuse him, but it was due to his presence that she survived.

They moved her to Hogarth House while she was still insane, and somehow found the wages for four living-in nurses. It was not until September 1915 that she could return to Asheham, still with a nurse, and began that slow process of rehabilitation that restored her to sanity for the next twenty-five years.

V

SO TRAUMATIC HAD been these experiences that Leonard, now a leading expert on international affairs, had barely noticed the outbreak of the European war. He was exempt from military service by the constant trembling of his hands. If he could not lift a cup without spilling it, a loaded rifle would have been more dangerous to his comrades than to the enemy. He was grateful for this relief, for to abandon Virginia would almost certainly have led her to fresh attempts at suicide, and in any case, he was half won over by the pacifist arguments of his friends. All Bloomsbury were conscientious objectors, on moral more than political grounds. When hauled before tribunals to affirm their motives, they would say that they totally disapproved of war as an instrument of policy, except Keynes, who considered that as the war was now a fact of life, it should be run as efficiently as possible. Clive Bell published a pamphlet called *Peace at Once*, which was destroyed on orders of the Lord Mayor of London for the defeatist arguments it proclaimed. Clive took a logical position: better surrender than allow the carnage to continue. Leonard did not go so far. While maintaining that it was a 'senseless and useless war', he hoped that we would win it. But he expressed no admiration for the soldiers who alone could win it, and broke completely with friends like Rupert Brooke, who went off to the Dardanelles with a song in his heart, writing to Violet Asquith, 'Oh Violet, I could not imagine that fate could be so benign. Oh God, I have never been quite so happy in my life.'

Virginia's attitude was different from Leonard's. She made no attempt to argue her case. To her the greatest war in history which killed ten million young men was an irrelevance. It simply confirmed her suspicion of a man-dominated society. It was 'a preposterous masculine fiction'; patriotism was 'a base emotion'. Let them fight if they must, but they were behaving 'like some curious tribe in central Africa'. When one of Leonard's brothers was killed and another severely wounded, all she wrote in her diary was, 'On Sunday we heard of Cecil's death and Philip's wounds', without a word of the pity she undoubtedly felt. She slept night after night in the cellar of Hogarth House, sheltering from the air raids, and although she mentioned these events in her diary, she never commented on them. She maintained an attitude to the war of complete indifference. Having no role in it herself, she would not bother to record it. Of the great battles in France – the very sound of the gunfire penetrated to Asheham – of America's entry into the war and the Russian Revolution, she wrote nothing in her letters or diary. But the war left an impact on her. In Virginia's later books, *Jacob's Room* and *The Years*, there are images of war, just as we can hear the distant boom of naval bombardment in Jane Austen's *Persuasion*.

Bloomsbury took to farming in the war, as the only alternative to fighting acceptable to the authorities and themselves. Ottoline Morrell provided such a refuge at Garsington for Lytton Strachey and Clive among others, with minimal labour attached. Duncan Grant, who had replaced Roger Fry in Vanessa's affections, and David ('Bunny') Garnett, who was in love with Duncan, worked at first on a fruit farm in Suffolk, until Virginia made a move on their behalf which changed their lives. She discovered Charleston. It was a roomy

Sussex farmhouse lying on the north side of the Downs near Firle, and she persuaded Vanessa to take a long lease of it. The two men could work out their war service in the local farm. The trio, with Vanessa's two sons, moved there in October 1916, and Clive, as titular husband and father, was treated as a welcome guest and had his permanent rooms there. Roger Fry wrote of this strange ménage, 'It really is almost an ideal family, based as it is on adultery and mutual forebearance, with Clive the deceived husband and me the abandoned lover. It really is rather a triumph of reasonableness over the conventions.' Charleston remained Vanessa's and Duncan's house until they died, and has since become the most enduring memorial of Bloomsbury's art, energy, relationships and taste.

Nearly three years had been taken out of Virginia's and Leonard's lives by her illnesses, and they emerged chastened, poor and eager for fresh enterprise. Their resilience was remarkable. She resumed her journalism, and Leonard was increasingly involved in Fabian and Labour Party politics. They alternated between Asheham and London, where Virginia took lessons in Italian and kept in touch with her friends, of whom the one who came to mean most to her was Lytton Strachey. She wrote of him in her diary, 'He is the most sympathetic and understanding friend to talk to. ... If one adds his peculiar flavour of mind, his wit and infinite intelligence, he is a figure not to be replaced.' Wartime duties had dispersed Bloomsbury (Virginia was now regularly using the term as a collective noun), but a nucleus remained in the Omega Workshop, which Roger Fry had founded to give employment to young artists and to experiment with the decorative arts, ranging from simple boxes to entire rooms.

Leonard's interests were not Virginia's, but from time to time she accompanied him on his political excursions, which were not always to her taste. Of Mrs Sidney Webb, the Fabian Socialist, she wrote, 'She pounces on one, rather like a moulting eagle, with a bald neck and bloodstained beak.' When Leonard became Secretary to the Labour Party's Committees on International and Imperial Affairs, and a deeply committed Socialist, she thought it behoved her to contribute some of her own ideas. 'V. said we ought to give up all our capital', he noted in his diary. 'I said it was nonsense.' Undismayed, she took the chair of the Richmond Branch of the Women's Cooperative Guild, and held monthly meetings at which lectures were given by her friends to audiences which often numbered as few as twelve. It was like Morley College again, but with a change of subject. When she proposed a lecture on venereal disease, her women were deeply shocked. Virginia persisted with the chore for two years. There was no doubting the genuineness of her wish to understand the mentality of the working class, nor the nobility of her failure, but it could not be an activity central to her life. She had already embarked on her second novel, *Night and Day*.

In his autobiography, Leonard described how profoundly she immersed herself in her work, and the passage is worth quoting, for nobody knew better than him what her writing cost her in mental stress:

I have never known anyone work with more intense, more indefatigable, concentration than Virginia. This was particularly the case when she was writing a novel. The novel became part of her, and she herself was absorbed into the novel. She wrote only in the morning from 10 till 1, and usually she typed out in the afternoon what she had written by hand in the morning, but all day long, when she was walking through London streets or on the Sussex Downs, the book would be moving subconsciously in her mind, or she herself would be moving in a dreamlike way through the book. It was this intense absorption which made writing so mentally exhausting for her.

Leonard decided, with her full agreement, that Virginia needed a diversion, apart from walks and parties. Instead of proposing gardening or knitting, he revived an earlier idea to buy a printing press. 'It would take her mind completely off her work', he considered. He intended it not so much as therapy, to avert another mental attack, but as a recreation. They both thought of it that way, but as they decided that they would print and sell booklets, it was a more ambitious venture than a hobby, though Virginia once used that word to describe it. They were amateurs at the trade, but dedicated. They taught themselves, with the aid of a brochure and a friendly printer at Richmond Green, how to operate the handpress which they bought in April 1917 and put in the drawing-room at Hogarth House. After much labour, they issued their first booklet, *Two Stories*, of which one was by Leonard, and the other, *The Mark on the Wall*, by Virginia, illustrated with woodcuts by the Slade student, Dora Carrington, and sold it to their friends under their own imprint, the Hogarth Press, for one shilling and sixpence a copy. They printed 150 copies, and when twenty-seven were left, Leonard upped the price to two shillings. He intended to be not only a printer-publisher, but a businessman. Clive gave a copy to my mother before she had ever met Virginia. I treasured it after Vita's death, but was foolish enough to boast to a group of tourists that a copy had recently been sold at auction for £8,500. Two days later it was missing from Vita's bookshelves. I never saw it again.

Their difficulties were formidable. Leonard had chosen an occupation which required the handling of very small pieces of metal, a task impossible for a man whose hands trembled so violently, and he allotted it to Virginia, for whom it was certainly no rest-cure. She stood for hours sorting out the 'm's from 'n's, and arranged them on a printer's rule letter by letter, line by line, and when she had completed five lines, she handed them to Leonard who imposed them on his little machine. They could not print more than two pages at a time because they must reuse the type, being unable to afford to buy more. Virginia would take the text to pieces, inky though it was, and distribute the letters into their proper slots so that the process could be started all over again. Their earliest products were disfigured by incompetence. The typography was ugly, the printing and inking unequal, and the paper jackets often fell apart.

Unpredictably, Virginia enjoyed it. 'You can't think how exciting, soothing, ennobling and satisfying it is', she wrote to Margaret Llewelyn-Davies, and the adjectives were well chosen. It was not only the printing but the binding, of which she had had some practice as a child, that delighted her. For Leonard there was the additional pleasure of mastering a technique and organizing a business. He prided himself justifiably on having started the enterprise on a capital of only £20 (the cost of the handpress, type and essential tools) and sustained it for years on no further injection of money than was generated by sales. They had next to no overheads because their office was their house, they took no salaries for themselves, and when they began to employ assistants like Barbara Hiles and Ralph Partridge, they paid them a minimum wage. From the very start the Hogarth Press made a nominal profit.

Equally novel was their decision to publish poems and pamphlets that no commercial publisher would touch, and sell them exclusively by subscription. Leonard hoped to find a market for a new generation of writers, as Fry had fostered young artists by founding the Omega Workshop. The Woolfs could also publish their own books without having to endure the comments of outsiders like Gerald Duckworth. The third book issued by the Press was Katherine Mansfield's sixty-eight-page story *Prelude*, the fourth was T.S. Eliot's *Poems*, the fifth Virginia's *Kew Gardens*, and in 1920 E.M. Forster's *The Story of the Siren*. They limited themselves at first to two books a year, and when these were modestly successful, in 1921 they bought, at second-hand, a much larger press, a Minerva platen machine, operated by a foot-treadle. On this they printed Eliot's *The Waste Land*, 'which had a greater influence on English poetry,' Leonard remarked, 'indeed upon English literature, than any other book in the 20th century'. Virginia set the whole poem with her own hands, and Leonard printed it. At first it did not do well. Six months after publication, it had sold only 330 copies, on which the Press made a profit of £21 and Eliot earned £7. It was on this modest scale that it all began. Nobody knows what happened to the original handpress. It may have been thrown away. After printing a score more books on the platen machine, Leonard sold it to my mother in 1930, and it still stands, an inert chunk of metal like a medieval instrument of torture, in the oasthouse at Sissinghurst.

I must not exaggerate the pleasure that the Woolfs derived from the Press. It is true that its success is one of the legends of publishing. From its amateurish start it developed into a professional publishing firm which survives to this day. But instead of giving them an amusing recreation, like the flute-playing of Frederick the Great, it imposed on them endless chores. Virginia was obliged to spend hours of her time distributing and setting type, and reading other people's manuscripts when she longed to be writing her own, and there were inevitable misunderstandings with authors and artists. More than once they considered abandoning it ('It's worse than six children at the breast simultaneously', Virginia wrote in a moment of despair), but they never did.

Before acquiring *The Waste Land* they were offered James Joyce's *Ulysses*, its equal in audacity, but turned it down, partly because it would have taken them two years to set the type at their snail's pace and Leonard could find no commercial printer willing to risk prosecution for obscenity, and partly because Virginia herself found it distasteful. She thought it 'interesting as an experiment', but as she wrote to Nick Bagenal, 'I should hesitate to put it into the hands of Barbara [his wife] even though she is a married woman. The directness of the language and the choice of incidents ... have raised a blush even upon such a cheek as mine.' It is the only recorded occasion when Virginia admitted that a book was more scatological than she could stomach. It has been said that she changed her mind on rereading it. I can find no evidence of this. In 1922 she wrote to Lytton, 'Never did I read such tosh. As for the first two chapters we will let them pass, but the 3rd, 4th, 5th, 6th – merely the scratching of pimples on the body of the bootboy at Claridges'. The book that the

Hogarth Press was never offered, and would most have liked, was Strachey's own *Eminent Victorians*, published in May 1918, which surprisingly made acceptable to a wide public Bloomsbury's deflationary attitude to pre-war heroes.

From Virginia's diaries and letters we can know what she was doing almost every day. The diary was to her like a hammock, for contemplation; the letters were like a trampoline, for literary exercise and gossip. The dominant tone of the diary was melancholy; of the letters, provocation and delight. She showed the diary to no one, and many of the letters must have been put away after a single reading. They are evidence of how extraordinarily full her life had become in the closing years of the war. She was busy with the Cooperatives, and constantly entertaining and being entertained. She was writing the last chapters of *Night and Day* without any of the labour and self-distrust that had brought her first novel to birth. She thought it 'a much more mature and finished and satisfactory book' than *The Voyage Out*, but later told Leonard that she wrote it 'as a kind of exercise', to show that she could write a traditional novel before experimenting with *Jacob's Room*. She said, 'I've never enjoyed any writing so much as I did the last half of *Night and Day*', but she barely mentioned it in her diary and almost never in her letters while she was writing it. One is given an occasional hint. On Armistice Day, 11 November 1918, she wrote to Vanessa, 'How am I to write my last chapter with all this shindy', the shindy being Richmond's victory celebrations outside Hogarth House. Most of her correspondence is about who has married, or is likely to marry, the beauty of the Sussex Downs, or descriptions of parties in the 1917 Club where left-wing politicians met young artists and intellectuals, or abuse of friends, affectionately or semi-maliciously, like her description of Will Arnold-Forster, whom she was determined to dislike because he had married Ka Cox, 'His mongrel cur's body, his face which appears powdered and painted like a very refined old suburban harlot's.' Or take this account of dining alone with Ottoline Morrell:

It was a frigid success. The poor woman has broken out into eruptions which she tries to make dramatic by pasting pieces of black plaster on them – but they exude at the edges. It is a terrific business whipping her into life now. One has to bow and scrape and do all sorts of antics. ... When she said that I dressed so beautifully that I made her feel older and uglier than ever, I said, 'My dear Ottoline, like the Lombardy poplar you have only to stand up naked to put us all to shame.' She liked that.

These sallies were unkind. But they were written to amuse Vanessa for half a minute, not generations of scholars for a century.

It was to Vanessa that she most frequently wrote at this period, although for weeks at a time they lived only four miles apart. There was a certain defensiveness in Virginia's fencing with her sister, as if she was nervous of losing her. They had had a slight tiff over the reproduction of her woodcuts in *Kew Gardens*, and Vanessa had said that she wondered whether the Hogarth Press should not be given up; professional printers produced books so much better. This hurt Virginia. To her

Vanessa Bell in 1918 by Duncan Grant. To Virginia, 'Vanessa was a goddess, pagan "but with a natural piety", a madonna capable of bawdiness, sometimes mysteriously withdrawn, but vigorous, competent, serene.' National Portrait Gallery.

Vanessa was a goddess, pagan but 'with a natural piety', a madonna capable of bawdiness, sometimes mysteriously withdrawn but vigorous, competent, serene. She was valiant and strong, a magnet to attract the few she loved and to repel the many she found wanting. And she was a mother, now threefold. On Christmas Day 1918, a daughter was born to her at Charleston, to be named Angelica. She was not Clive's child, but Duncan's, as all Bloomsbury knew or surmised, except Angelica herself, who was not told the truth about her paternity until she was seventeen. In later life she wrote of her mother, 'Even if she said little, there emanated from her an enormous power, a pungency like the smell of crushed sage.'

It is something of a mystery how the Woolfs managed to spend so much money while earning so little. Leonard was now a prolific writer on international affairs and for some time he edited *The International Review*, but his fees and salary were exiguous. *Night and Day*, although it received excellent reviews, earned more for its publisher, Gerald Duckworth, than for its author. Her journalism brought in annually about £100. In its first four years the Hogarth Press's total net profit was £90. A little more was added by interest on Virginia's investments. But how did they manage on this income to keep two houses going in London and the country? That was not all. They rented for £15 a year three cottages in Cornwall which D.H. Lawrence had occupied during the war, and Leonard bought the freehold of Hogarth House and the house adjoining it for £1,950. Asheham was required by its landlord to house his bailiff, and they were obliged to give up the tenancy. Virginia, on impulse, bought the Round House (the stump of a windmill) in central Lewes for £300. There is no evidence that they ever spent a night in it, nor in the Cornish cottages, because in June 1919 they discovered Monk's House in the village of Rodmell, five miles from Lewes. They sold the Round House at a small profit, and bid successfully for Monk's House at the auction. It cost them £700.

Monk's House, and Charleston, its sister-house, have become more closely identified with Bloomsbury than any other buildings that survive. Vanessa and Duncan lived at Charleston until their deaths, while Monk's was Virginia's country home for the rest of her life, and Leonard's until he died in 1969. Both houses have been restored to more or less the condition that they knew, Charleston retaining many of its original decorations and paintings and Monk's its furniture. It was there, alternating with London, that Virginia wrote all her novels except the first two, and the simplicity of it is an indication of her taste and character.

It was not a beautiful house, and very uncomfortable. When they moved in from Asheham in September 1919, loading their books and furniture on two farm carts, like the Brontës on moving from Thornton to Haworth, there was no running water, no electricity, no bath, an evil-smelling earth-closet in the loft and only an oil stove to cook upon. The house had no extensive views from its windows, and its garden was a jungle. But it was the potential beauty of the orchard that made the greatest appeal to both of them, and the lawn from which they could look across the valley of the Ouse to the Downs. It was the last house on the lane that led down to the river. They could work undisturbed except for the tolling of the church bell and the shouts of small children in the school.

Very cautiously they made improvements, and risked

friendships by inviting guests to stay a night before the improvements were ready, but it was one of the pleasantest characteristics of Bloomsbury that they never craved luxury or complained of discomfort. Monk's House would never rate more than one star for bed and breakfast. I remember it in the Woolfs' days as a simple place, rather larger than a cottage, rather smaller than a house, not shabby exactly, but untidy, with saucers of pet food left on the floor and books on each tread of the narrow staircase. When they began to make money by Virginia's books, they added some amenities (the water-closet was named after Mrs Dalloway), but Leonard was no architect, and when *Orlando* made possible an annexe for Virginia's bedroom, he built it with no direct access from the house, no bathroom and no lavatory, and the gardener would gaze at her through the window as she lay in bed. They both lacked visual taste. The only objects to please the eye were chairs and tables from Omega and Vanessa's tiles around the fireplaces. Even the garden, which was Leonard's delight, was conceived by him on too grand a scale, with ornamental pools, urns and statues. Virginia once asked my mother what she thought of it, and Vita rather hesitantly replied, 'You can't recreate Versailles on a quarter-acre of Sussex. It just cannot be done.' Virginia acquired a wooden hut and put it in a corner of the garden from where she had a view of Mount Caburn. There she wrote her books during the summer months. After her death it was doubled in size for a studio. It should be halved again, to restore its shape and character.

In April 1920 she began to write her third novel, *Jacob's Room*, her first truly experimental book. It was 'the things one doesn't say', the art of suggesting important truths by deviousness, that she now began to explore, the delineation of character not by direct description but by the behaviour of other people around them. She wrote to a new friend, Gerald Brenan, in one of the few letters where she discussed her work, 'The human soul, it seems to me, orientates itself afresh every now and then. It is doing so now. No one can see it whole, therefore. The best of us catch a glimpse of a nose, a shoulder, something turning away, always in movement. Still, it seems better to me to catch this glimpse, than to sit down with Hugh Walpole, Wells etc etc, and make large oil paintings of fabulous fleshy monsters complete from top to toe.' Other writers were too conventional or too frivolous, even Lytton Strachey, whose *Queen Victoria* she admired with reservations. 'I think one is a little conscious of being entertained', she wrote to him. 'It's a little too luxurious reading – I mean, one is willing perhaps to take more pains than you allow.' She had put her finger on the spot, gently, and then lifted it again. When Lytton asked if he might dedicate the book to her, she agreed, insisting on 'Virginia Woolf', not just 'V.W.', in case some Victoria Worms or Vincent Woodhouse would snatch the compliment from her.

The only writer for whom she felt acute jealousy was Katherine Mansfield. They were attempting to transform fiction in the same sort of way, and Virginia sometimes suspected that Katherine was the more successful. In character, they were opposites. Katherine, a New Zealander, six years younger than Virginia, was abrasive more than provocative, sexually more audacious, less anxious to impress and please, alarming, vulgar even. While Virginia was capable of hurting people's feelings and then regretted it, Katherine didn't care:

she would do it again. She could be as envious of Virginia as Virginia was of her. While courteous to each other when they met, they were highly critical when apart. In reviewing *Night and Day*, Katherine called it 'old-fashioned', 'reeking with snobbery', which deeply hurt Virginia, and she decided, but only in the privacy of her diary, that their friendship 'was almost entirely founded on quicksands'. She admitted her jealousy ('the more she is praised, the more I am convinced that she is bad'), but when Katherine died of tuberculosis in 1923, aged thirty-four, Virginia wrote movingly about her, expressing relief that she had 'a rival the less', but, 'it seemed to me that there is no point in writing: Katherine won't read it'. They had stimulated, angered, each other, flint against stone. When Joanne Trautmann and I were editing Virginia's letters, we searched despairingly for her letters to Katherine, as their correspondence would probably be the most important in both their lives, but we found only one letter of three lines, a false note of congratulations on Katherine's *Bliss*. When Professor Trautmann was editing the one-volume edition of the letters, which she called *Congenial Spirits*, she was able to include one other, much longer letter, in which Virginia complimented Katherine on her style: 'You seem to me to go so straightly and directly – all clear as glass – refined, spiritual', while to Janet Case, a year later, she castigated it: 'I read *Bliss*, and it was so brilliant – so hard, and so shallow, and so sentimental that I had to rush to the bookcase for something to drink', by which she meant Shakespeare. It was a difficult relationship, with love and envy on both sides.

In these post-war years Bloomsbury gathered itself together again. Thirteen of them formed a society called the Memoir Club, which endured until 1956, the younger members replacing those who died. Its purpose was strange: to read to each other recollections of their youth. The papers were written to entertain, and truth was frequently sacrificed to fantasy. When some of them were published many years later, the qualifications and note of ribaldry were missing. Virginia's unkind account of George Duckworth, for example, has ever since stained the reputation of that conventional but fundamentally decent man. In public Bloomsbury had much to be reticent about, though certainly not ashamed. They had settled into separate but intercommunicating pools. There were the Woolfs at Rodmell, so happy together that Virginia considered that there was no more contented couple in the country. There was Garsington, where Ottoline Morrell offered Bloomsberries generous hospitality, only to be rewarded by their ridicule, though Virginia, who was not slow to join in, would admit to Ottoline's 'fundamental integrity' and 'an element of the superb'. There was the Mill at Tidmarsh, where Lytton Strachey cohabited with Carrington, who loved him, while he loved Ralph Partridge, who was to marry her. And there was Charleston, the hub of the entire circuit, where Vanessa presided with her lover Duncan Grant and David Garnett. It was when a cousin, Dorothea Stephen, expressed disapproval of Vanessa's morals and hesitated to meet her, that Virginia discarded her pen for a flame-thrower: 'I could not let you come here without saying that I entirely sympathise with Vanessa's view and conduct'. It was not just loyalty to a sister. It was confirmation that Bloomsbury people could live with whomever they chose, whatever their sex, because they loved them, and that was more moral than continuing for propriety's sake to live with someone whom you had ceased to love in any meaningful way.

From time to time Virginia was too ill to work. In the summer of 1921 she was so often bedridden with fluctuating headaches and sleeplessness, symptoms of an approaching breakdown, that she sometimes feared that she had not long to live. When she recovered from these spasms, she usually convalesced in Cornwall, and on returning to London would immediately resume her social life. She never moped. She expressed self-distrust but never self-pity. Much as she loved the quietness of Rodmell, she enticed her friends to visit her there, and in London scarcely had a meal alone with Leonard. When invited out, her defiance of convention was forgiven for the sake of the brilliance of her talk. Dining with Nellie Cecil, 'I said all the most impossible things in a very loud voice . . . abused Lady Glenconner, and then attacked Rupert Brooke: but at my age and with my habits, how conform to the way of the world? Hairpins dropped steadily into my soup-plate: I gave them a lick, and put them in again.' When she chose, she could be decorous, and rather enjoyed high society, but it was at supper in Hogarth House with Eliot or Strachey when she felt most content.

She was a generous person, not so much with money, for she had little to spare, but with her time and patience. She wrote long letters to Jacques Raverat because he was dying of multiple sclerosis. She did her utmost to save T.S. Eliot from the drudgery of working in a bank when he could be writing immortal poetry. With Ezra Pound and Ottoline Morrell she organized an Eliot Fund, appealing to her friends to donate £10 a year towards his upkeep, but Bloomsbury was poor, and suspected that Pound might spend their £10 on drink, so that the fund never topped £100, and Eliot, squirming with embarrassment, suddenly declared that he must be guaranteed £500 a year for five years before he could consider leaving the bank. Virginia's campaign had been heroic. She disliked asking friends for money as much as he disliked receiving it, and she confessed in her diary that she wished Eliot had more spunk in him. They wound up the fund, giving him a paltry £50, but that was not the limit of Virginia's efforts on his behalf. She tried to persuade Maynard Keynes, who had taken control of the *Nation*, the highbrow weekly, to offer Eliot the literary editorship, but after much shilly-shallying he refused it, and the job was given, to their surprise, to Leonard.

The Woolfs' careers were now in full spate. Leonard stood for Parliament, and to their joint relief failed to be elected. The Hogarth Press never wavered in its ascent from obscurity. When Ralph Partridge was eased out by Leonard for insufficient dedication to the Press, they hired George (Dadie) Rylands to take his place, but the work imposed on the two founders was still crushing. Having spent most afternoons setting type and machining it, they would set out for the bookshops, attempting to sell their wares to a mostly indifferent trade, and even toyed with the idea of opening a bookshop or picture gallery of their own.

Their most provocative new publication was Virginia's *Jacob's Room*. It puzzled the literary world. Its treatment of fiction was so original that critics hesitated to abuse it for fear that they might be overlooking a masterpiece. It was not a consecutive narrative, but more like a shuffled pack of cards or slides for a lecture arranged in no logical order. Virginia explained that it was an 'experiment', which she intended to develop in her next book, and before long she started to write *Mrs Dalloway*, finding it immensely difficult, and to put in order some of her past essays for *The Common Reader*.

Her concentration on her own work never dulled her interest in other people's. She was teaching herself Russian in order to help Samuel Koteliansky with his translations of Tolstoy's love letters. She continued to study Homer. She discovered the novels of Rebecca West, whom she had never met, 'a brave, clever woman', she decided, 'who sometimes writes a few words very nicely', which from Virginia was high praise. Proust, whose great work she was steadily absorbing, left her 'in a state of amazement, as if a miracle were being done before my eyes. One has to put the book down and gasp.' She thought Anthony Trollope's *The Small House at Allington* 'perhaps the most perfect of English novels'. She even found time for the Old Testament, but it could not compete with Proust. 'I don't think God comes well out of it', was her comment on the Book of Job.

In April 1923 they went abroad for the first time since their honeymoon in 1912. They travelled through France and Spain to Madrid and Granada, and continued by bus and mule to Yegen, a remote village in the Sierra Nevada where Gerald Brenan, ex-soldier and romantic, had isolated himself in a small cottage to study great works of literature, and, if possible, add to them himself. Out of friendship for him, Ralph Partridge had induced Lytton to visit him in the previous year, and Carrington, now Ralph's wife, went with them. No man was less suited to arduous travel than Lytton Strachey. He suffered terribly. The oil-soaked Spanish food upset his stomach. Their journey, at first by bus, then by cart, finally by mules zigzagging up the mountain tracks or wallowing belly-deep in swollen rivers, utterly exhausted him. When they finally reached Brenan's cottage, he found that the only lavatory was a board with a hole in it poised over the chicken-run. Then Carrington and Brenan fell in love. It was too much. All this he related to Virginia as a warning, but it did not deter her. Everyone considered her too fragile to attempt such an ordeal, but she loved it. Unhappily, her diary of the expedition is lost, but we have Brenan's tribute in his book *South from Granada* that 'though quiet, she was as excited as a schoolgirl'. She spent ten days with him, and three days in Paris on their return. She spared her friends any account of her achievement. 'How dull travellers' stories are!', she wrote to Molly MacCarthy as a caution to all of us. 'I omit all about the adventures, with the mule, the vulture, and the wolf. Your imagination can play freely upon them.'

VI

FROM MURCIA IN Spain Virginia wrote to Vita Sackville-West, my mother. They had met for the first time only a few months before. Her letter was to refuse Vita's suggestion that Virginia might care to join the PEN Club, an international literary society which discussed not so much literature as authors. Virginia's letter was kindly expressed but in effect it was a snub. Vita had misunderstood her character. She thought that because Bloomsbury was a sort of society, Virginia must be clubbable, and would enjoy discussing with other writers, most of whom would be strangers to her, the difficulties of their trade. It was a curious mistake for Vita to have made, because she herself was equally secretive about her writing. It seemed that her bloomer would put an end to their friendship scarcely before it had begun.

They had met in December 1922, dining with Clive Bell, and four days later Vita invited her to dinner with Clive and Desmond MacCarthy. From Vita's point of view, the party was a great success. She wrote to my father, 'I simply adore Virginia Woolf, and so would you. You would fall quite flat before her charm and personality. She is utterly unaffected. She dresses quite atrociously. I've rarely taken such a fancy to anyone.' Virginia's account of Vita in her diary was less flattering: 'Not much to my severer taste – florid, moustached, parakeet coloured, with all the supple ease of the aristocracy, but not the wit of the artist.' All the same, she invited Vita to Hogarth House, and their friendship, if not their intimacy, grew: 'Dined with Virginia at Richmond. She is as delicious as ever.' 'Lunched with her in Tavistock Square, where she had just arrived. Went on to see Mama [Lady Sackville], my head swimming with Virginia.' Her admiration was not yet reciprocated, and then came the PEN episode, which nearly put a stop to it.

They were reaching out to touch with fingertips what can only be grasped by the whole hand, leaving time and space for retreat if either of them came to regret it. It took two years

Vita Sackville-West, a photograph by Lenare taken in 1927 during her short affair with Virginia. 'Here we have Vita, exceedingly bold at one moment, and exceedingly shy at the next, falling in love with Virginia, ten years older than herself, and scared of her.'

for their friendship to develop into intimacy, and three for intimacy to be acknowledged on both sides as love. It was so unlikely a friendship that their biographers have all reached different interpretations of it. Here we have Vita, exceedingly bold at one moment and exceedingly shy at the next, falling in love with Virginia, ten years older than herself, and scared of her. Bloomsbury was too clever for her, and deliberately alarming to strangers. 'Ever heard of Moore?', Virginia asked Vita. 'You mean George Moore, the novelist?' 'No, no, no – G.E. Moore, the philosopher', of whom Vita had never heard. Early in their relationship, Vita and my father were invited to dine in Gordon Square with Virginia, Leonard, Vanessa, Duncan Grant, Clive and Lytton Strachey. It was all too obviously designed as an occasion to inspect Virginia's new friend. Lytton sneered at my father's life of Tennyson (published on that very day), and Harold, recoiling from his contempt, relapsed into silence. In sympathy, so did Vita. Two days later Virginia wrote in her diary, 'It was a rocky steep evening. . . . We judged them both incurably stupid.'

Harold was not a stupid man, but Vita, when ill at ease, could be slow-witted. When she was at her writing-table, ideas pullulated from her brain as if from a cornucopia, but in company with more than one or two people, her conversation was apt to be halting. She lacked the gift of repartee: she could not turn a challenging question to her own advantage, an art at which Bloomsbury excelled. What's more, in their eyes she was old-fashioned. Her pastoral poem *The Land* was contrasted with *The Waste Land* (the very titles pointing up the difference) and found wanting. She had no taste for classical music, and thought Duncan's and Vanessa's panels in Tavistock Square 'of inconceivable hideousness'. It is not surprising that Vanessa considered Vita 'an unnecessary importation into our society', and was astonished by Virginia's growing intimacy with her, if not actually jealous. 'Has your Vita gone?', she once wrote to her sister. 'Don't expend all your energies on writing to her. I consider that I have first claim.'

What, then, caused this uneasy relationship to develop into a love-affair? What was Vita's attraction for Virginia? In the first place, Vita had had a fruitier past. There was her ancestry, and the Sackvilles' great house, Knole, which aroused Virginia's historical senses like the smell of pot-pourri in an antique bowl, but not, I think, her snobbishness, since she had no use for the aristocracy unless, like David Cecil, they also possessed the qualities she sought in other people. Vita herself had reacted against her family's traditions, while honouring them. It was her *Knole and the Sackvilles* that had first caught Virginia's attention. But Vita refused to play the role expected of the only child of so great a dynasty. From the age of fourteen, without any encouragement from her parents, she had written plays and full-length romances with astonishing exuberance, some of them in French and Italian, which she spoke fluently. She was indifferent to the playmates whom her mother enticed to Knole for tea parties: she locked them up in the toolshed, and stifled their cries of protest by stuffing their noses with putty. As she grew to débutante age, she was very beautiful, dark and lustrous, and was courted by 'every little dancing thing in London', as she described them. She could have been châtelaine of Belvoir or Harewood, houses as famous as Knole itself, but she chose to marry Harold Nicolson, a penniless third secretary in the Foreign Office.

That was not all. While still an adolescent, she recognized

in herself an attraction towards her own sex rather than to boys and men. She had a sentimental love-affair with a foolish girl called Rosamund Grosvenor, and then dropped her for Violet Trefusis, daughter of Alice Keppel, Edward VII's mistress. Only a year or two before she met Virginia she eloped with Violet to France, to be retrieved by their two husbands in a dramatic scene at Amiens which has become, in print and film, a notorious incident in the history of the British upper classes.

All this Virginia knew, and was impressed by it. There was the further attraction that Vita was also a writer, better-known in 1922 than Virginia herself, for besides her early novels, she was a poet too, and a critic good enough to be judged by Leonard worthy to contribute regular book reviews to the *Nation*. They could discuss literature together not on equal terms, for Vita acknowledged Virginia's superior gift, which Virginia did not trouble to deny, but with a common background in the literature of the past, and they corresponded endlessly. The letters of one took fire from the other's. How much more entertaining were Virginia's letters to Vita than those she had written to Violet Dickinson, and Vita's to Virginia than those to another Violet. There were occasions when Virginia could not suppress admiration for Vita's writing. 'A pen of brass', was her dismissive verdict to Jacques Raverat, which is often quoted to indicate her contempt, but it was not typical. She saw in *The Land* a talent of which she was incapable, in *Seducers in Ecuador* (which she published) a cleverness which she could hardly have suspected from Vita's conversation, and of *Passenger to Teheran* she wrote to Vita, 'Yes – I think it is awfully good. I didn't know the extent of your subtleties', and meant it. Vita, she discovered, had a 'rich, dusky attic of a mind'. In Victoria Glendinning's phrase about *Seducers*, Vita had 'out-Bloomsburied Bloomsbury'. In the same issue of the *New York Evening Post* it was reviewed jointly with *Mrs Dalloway*, but it was *Seducers* that headed the column with high commendation, while Virginia's book was considered more shortly as 'a fog of words'.

It was said that Vita was like a mother to Virginia, but I can find no evidence of this. Their relationship, though tentative at first, was always on the level, protective, perhaps, on Vita's side, but not maternal, nor submissive on Virginia's. They were mutually solicitous and provocative. Vita seemed astonished that Virginia should love her carnally (Virginia's word), and when in December 1925 they first slept together at Long Barn, Vita's house near Knole, it seems to have been as much on Virginia's initiative as on the more experienced Vita's. As Mitchell Leaska has astutely commented, 'Vita seemed forever fanning the embers of passion yet forever stepping back from its blaze.' She was flattered, naturally, but fearful of arousing in Virginia passions that might ignite a fresh attack of madness. 'For heaven's sake be careful', Harold warned her when she confessed to him. 'It's not merely playing with fire; it's playing with gelignite.' He need not have worried. Their affair continued, on and off, for about three years, without damaging either of them.

More puzzling is Virginia's attitude. She was not a deeply sensual woman. Her affection for Violet Dickinson and Madge Vaughan had been more sentimental than physical, but she confessed to herself that women attracted her more than men. Towards the end of 1924, when her friendship with Vita was intensifying, she wrote in her diary, 'If one could be friendly with women, what a pleasure – the relationship so secret and private compared with relations with men!' But when, a year later, after the Vita affair had begun, she asked herself who were essential to her happiness, she named six people – Leonard, Vanessa, Duncan, Clive, Lytton and E.M. Forster – only one of whom was a woman, and Vita was not mentioned at all. She expressed no fear, and no shame, in undertaking at the age of forty-three the only love-affair of her life. Rather, she was curious about her own reaction to it, as Vanessa was when Virginia told her about it one day when they were shopping, and Vanessa asked her how one woman could make love to another. Virginia did not record her reply, and worded her account of what was happening ambiguously, even in her diary. 'These Sapphists', she wrote, as if she were not one herself, 'love women. Friendship is never untinged with amorosity.' She found homosexual relations between men distasteful. 'Have you any views on loving one's own sex?', she asked Raverat. 'All the young men are so inclined, and I can't help finding it mildly foolish, though I have no particular reason. For one thing they all tend to the pretty and ladylike. They paint and powder. ... Then the ladies, either in self-protection, or in imitation or genuinely, are given to their sex too', and then follows a fanciful account of Vita's elopement with Violet, not to either woman's credit.

Does all this covering-up indicate that Virginia considered that she was doing wrong, or was it an attempt to minimize scandal about her and Vita? Undoubtedly she was anxious not to distress Leonard. When he heard of the affair, she laughed it off and told him not to worry. Their marriage was not threatened by it. If Harold did not mind (in fact he thought it would do Vita much good), nor should Leonard.

But the two marriages, though similar in several ways, were not identical. Leonard was not a homosexual like Harold, and he spent almost every day with Virginia, while Harold at the beginning and height of the affair was in Teheran at the British Legation. Vita wrote to him an almost daily commentary on it, telling him, 'One's love for Virginia is a very different thing, a mental thing, a spiritual thing if you like, an intellectual thing, and she inspires a feeling of tenderness which I suppose is because of the funny mixture of hardness and softness. . . . Also she loves me, which flatters and pleases me.' Then she added, 'I am scared to death of arousing physical feelings in her because of the madness'. Presumably Leonard cautioned Virginia too, but he seemed to be more bored than worried. It is not surprising that Vita saw Leonard as 'a funny, grim, solitary creature' in contrast to Virginia, who was an angel of wit and intelligence.

It was at this period that I first came to know her. In 1924 I was seven years old, and my brother Ben was nine. She often came to Long Barn for a night or two, and we greatly looked forward to her visits, being ignorant of their cause. (A woman, who should have known better, once said to me, 'You realise that Virginia loves your mother', to which I innocently replied, 'Yes, of course she does: we all do.') Virginia was not particularly fond of children apart from Vanessa's, and except for James in *To the Lighthouse*, they do not figure largely in her novels. But she was interested in us, because children, like eccentrics, are unusual people, and under the guise of amusing us she would amuse herself: 'Tell me, what have you done this morning?' 'Well, nothing much.' 'No, no, that won't do. What woke you up?' 'The sun, coming through our bedroom window.' 'Was it a happy sun or an angry sun?' We answered that somehow, and then it was dressing: 'Which sock did you put on first, right or left?' And breakfast, and so on, right up to the moment when we came to find her. It was a lesson in observation, but it was also a hint: 'Unless you catch ideas on the wing and nail them down, you will soon cease to have any.' It was advice that I was to remember all my life.

We did not think of her as famous: indeed, when we first knew her, she wasn't. She was more like a favourite aunt who brightened our simple lives with unexpected questions: 'What is the French mistress like? What sort of shoes does she wear? Can you smell her scent when she comes into the classroom?' Apart from the butterfly-hunting, she seemed to us an indoor person, autumnal more than summery, happiest when warming her hands at a log fire, and talking, talking, talking, in a deep, slightly sing-song voice, teasing, provocative, drawing back her hair from her forehead as if to clear her mind. It is with Long Barn that I mainly associate her, but we would often go to Knole, where she would lean S-curved against a doorway, finger to her chin, contemplative, amused. I do not remember thinking her beautiful, but children's taste is for prettiness not beauty. Although Vita exaggerated in saying that she dressed 'atrociously,' she cared little for her appearance, hating make-up and being fitted by shop assistants, and bought loose, unemphatic clothes off the peg, which draped around her like folded wings.

Occasionally Vita would take one of us to Monk's House when she was not staying the night there, and one incident remains very clearly in my memory. Besides Virginia and Leonard, the only people present were Keynes and his wife Lydia Lopokova, the ballerina. We sat in the larger of the two sitting-rooms, and the discussion (I forget what it was about)

Nigel (left) and Ben Nicolson with Virginia Woolf at Knole in 1928, when she was writing *Orlando*. 'She would lean S-curved against a doorway, finger to her chin, contemplative, amused.'

grew animated. Virginia, standing by the fireplace, was arguing excitedly, when Leonard slowly rose from his chair and gently touched her on the shoulder. Without enquiry or protest, she followed him from the room, and they were absent for about a quarter of an hour. Nobody made any comment when they returned, since everyone except myself knew exactly what had happened. In her excitement, Virginia might overstep the bounds of sanity, and Leonard, observing her closely, took her away to calm down. When I read in some feminist accounts of their relationship allegations that Leonard neglected her, even drove her to suicide, I think of that incident. The gesture with which he touched her on the shoulder was almost biblical in its tenderness, and her submission to him indicated a trust that she awarded to no other person.

VII

IN MARCH 1924 they left Richmond for 52 Tavistock Square in Bloomsbury, dragging the Hogarth Press with them. The move was dictated by Leonard's desire to live closer to his work, and Virginia's for the society of her friends. Hogarth House was too remote. But their new house lacked the calm of Richmond. It was a sandwich, the Woolfs occupying the two top floors and the Press the basement, the offices of a solicitor lying between them. Virginia chose to write in a back room next to the Press, sitting in a moulting armchair with a board on her knee, and as it was also the stockroom, she was constantly interrupted by the assistants, who succeeded each other in quick rotation, such was Leonard's severity as an employer and so poor the pay. Even Dadie Rylands, whom they both liked, fled back to Cambridge after a few months.

It was in these conditions that Virginia finished *Mrs Dalloway*. It made great demands on her, particularly when she was describing the madness and suicide of Septimus Warren Smith. It was published in April 1925, a few weeks after *The Common Reader*. The two books were inevitably contrasted by the critics, the novel arousing bewilderment for its deliberate mistiness, 'the half-light of experience', the essays praise for their lucidity and wit. Vita, not wishing to offend or to be considered stupid, settled for 'will-of-the-wisp' for *Mrs Dalloway* and 'a guide, philosopher and friend' for *The Common Reader*. Virginia considered that hardly anyone had grasped her intention, 'but that's the penalty we pay for breaking with tradition'. Lytton Strachey thought the novel flawed, and Virginia, always vulnerable to criticism, felt more inclined to trust his judgment than Clive Bell's, who declared it to be a masterpiece, as did E.M. Forster and Jacques Raverat, who read the proofs as he lay dying, and dictated to his wife a letter which gave Virginia 'one of the happiest days of my life'. For many readers *Mrs Dalloway* meant too much hard work. Arnold Bennett admitted in a review, 'It beat me; I could not finish it'. In her famous essay, 'Mr Bennett and Mrs Brown', which she adapted as a lecture to a Cambridge literary society, Virginia answered him, explaining that she had hoped to change the whole direction of fiction-writing. She had already written in her diary: 'The method of writing smooth narrative can't be right. Things don't happen in one's mind like that. We experience, all the time, an overlapping of images and ideas, and modern novels should convey our mental confusion instead of neatly rearranging it. The reader must sort it out.' Less sophisticated readers were unconvinced. In reply to Violet Dickinson's letter of despair, Virginia advised her to give it up, and that was the end of that relationship.

She made new friends warily: Raymond Mortimer, Hugh Walpole, Vita's first cousin Edward Sackville-West. She could find little to admire in young men: she thought them insipid. Young women like Janet Vaughan, Rose Macaulay, Frances Marshall (Partridge to be), Carrington and Rebecca West had more spunk in them, more pride, and were less anxious to please. She and Leonard were increasingly reluctant to spend weekends away from home. They found it disagreeable to be under the constraint of other people's habits and hospitality, and to be forced to mix cordially with their neighbours. After one such winter visit to the Arnold-Forsters in Cornwall, Virginia thought it necessary, like many another weekend guest, to simulate the pleasure she had not felt. To Ka, her hostess, she wrote, 'I can't think how you manage such comfort and warmth in that howling blizzard': but to Vanessa, 'We fled from Zennor a day early, unable to stand the perishing cold'.

Monk's House was little better, but it was slowly acquiring the basic conveniences that they had lacked for seven years. 'Mrs Dalloway's lavatory' and hot water on tap were operating in time to comfort Virginia when she was obliged, once more, to spend months in bed with recurrent headaches. Her illnesses alternated with moves to London and back again, at the very period when she was longing to make progress with *To the Lighthouse*. When she was well enough to write, it came easily to her. 'I am now writing as fast and freely as I have written in the whole of my life', she confided to her diary when she was at Rodmell, but it was not the same in Tavistock Square. 'To write a novel in the heart of London', she told Vita, 'is next to an impossibility. I feel as if I were nailing a flag to the top of a mast in a raging gale.'

Vita was in Persia. In the years 1926 and 1927 she made two visits there, to join Harold in Teheran for a month or two, and her correspondence with Virginia gained on both sides a new intensity. They were not explicitly love-letters, for discretion's sake, but they were by implication. Virginia to Vita: 'No letter from you. Why not? Only a scrap from Dover, and a wild melancholy adorable moan from Trieste. No photograph either. Goodbye, dearest shaggy creature.' Vita to Virginia: 'It's incredible how essential to me you have become. Damn you, spoilt creature. I shan't make you love me any the more by giving myself away like this. But you have broken down my defences.' That was all very well. Vita was accompanied on both her journeys to the East by Dorothy Wellesley, another lover, and was writing ahead to Harold in Teheran letters as ardent as those she was writing back to Virginia in London. She did not consider it deceitful. She was simply sharing her affections between them. When she reached Teheran, having dumped Dorothy in India, she hardly mentioned her husband in her letters. She exchanged with Virginia common distastes, hers for smart diplomatic parties, Virginia's for their London equivalents, 'those damned people sitting smug round their urn, their fire, their tea-table. . . . I felt inclined to leave them all alone, for ever and ever, these tea-parties, these Ottolines, these mumbling sodomitical old maids.'

Such moods were frequent with her. Once she was persuaded by Leonard to spend a day with his brother Herbert and his wife, who lived at Cookham in Berkshire. Herbert was a stockbroker, lacking all intellectual interests, and Virginia, instead of ridiculing them as was her custom, reflected how comforting it would be never to have heard of Roger, or Clive, or Duncan, or Lytton. 'Oh this is life, I kept saying to myself; and what is Bloomsbury, or Long Barn either, but a contortion, a temporary knot;' she wrote to Vita, 'and why do I pity and deride the human race, when its lot is profoundly peaceful and happy? They have nothing to wish for. They are entirely simple and sane.'

It is doubtful whether Herbert mentioned the Stock Exchange or Leonard the problems of the Hogarth Press, for shop talk, by common convention, was taboo. Yet the Press was causing them much worry. They were still printing and binding pamphlets like Laura Riding's *Voltaire* and Robert Trevelyan's *Poems*. Longer books, like Virginia's own novels and Vita's *Passenger to Teheran*, they delegated to commercial printers, but their time, which Leonard would have preferred to devote to journalism, books and politics, and Virginia to her novels, was eroded by their mechanical tasks, packing parcels and interviewing booksellers and salesman. Was it worth this incessant drudgery? In 1927 their net profit was only £27. But they persisted. They considered buying David Garnett's bookshop, and publishing the works of Freud in translation. They abandoned Garnett, but Freud they carried through, though it is doubtful whether Virginia read a word of him.

The General Strike of May 1926 was more of an excitement than a diversion. The Hogarth Press was only marginally affected by it, because their sole employees, Angus Davidson and a secretary, did not strike, and printing by outside firms was interrupted only for the nine days that the strike lasted.

Leonard and Virginia Woolf at Monk's House in 1926, with Pinka
(Flush) in the foreground. A photograph taken by Vita.

take political sides. Hitherto she had been lukewarm. Now, in support of Leonard, she stood by the strikers, if not as valiantly as he did. 'If ever a general strike was justified', he wrote in his Memoirs, 'it was in 1926', and he organized in their support a petition by leading intellectuals which only Galsworthy refused to sign. The strike was suddenly settled, to the disadvantage of the miners who had started it. 'Everyone is jubilant', Virginia reported to Vanessa. 'We are going to have a strike dinner, and drink champagne with Clive, the Frys, and other spirits.' Her support for the strikers was couched in terms of dislike for authority, including the Prime Minister, Stanley Baldwin, whose radio appeal she thought ridiculous. She did not explain her reasons, not even in *A Room of One's Own*, where she quoted Baldwin's broadcast. She was as uncertain in her political judgments as Leonard was firm in his.

It was in the middle of this shindy that she wrote the magical chapter in *To the Lighthouse*, 'Time Passes'. On Vita's return from her first journey to Persia, their love-affair continued intermittently with exchange visits to Rodmell and Long Barn. Virginia was at heart more passionate, Vita on paper more outspoken. While Virginia could write in her diary, 'It is a spirited, creditable affair, I think innocent (spiritually) and all gain I think, rather a bore for Leonard, but not enough to worry him', there was no 'I think' in Vita's replies from Persia on her second visit in 1927: 'I always get devastated when I hear from you. God, I do love you. You say I use no endearments. That strikes me as funny, when I wake in the Persian dawn, and say to myself, "Virginia, Virginia"'.

After two months in Teheran ('God, the people here!', by whom she meant not the Persians but the diplomatists and their wives), she embarked with Harold and two friends on an arduous crossing of the Bakhtiari mountains to the Persian Gulf, the subject of her second book of Persian travels, *Twelve Days*. At the same time Virginia and Leonard were in Italy, loving it so much ('We found wild cyclamen and marble lapped by the water') that they thought of taking a villa in Rome's Campagna. Vita and Virginia reunited in May, exhilarated by work and travel. Each was buoyed up by success. *The Land* won the Hawthornden Prize, and *To the Lighthouse*, the Femina Prize, England's two most prestigious literary awards. The reviews of Virginia's book were favourable but cautious, as if the critics felt themselves to be on trial as much as the author, Arnold Bennett acknowledging that it was 'an improvement' on *Mrs Dalloway*, but he was still disconcerted by her fragmentary style, as was Aldous Huxley, who wrote that she had lost touch with the real world. Edwin Muir wrote of 'Time Passes', 'For imagination and beauty of writing it is probably not surpassed in contemporary prose'. But the verdict which Virginia most anxiously awaited was Vanessa's. The book was written in recollection of their childhood holidays in Cornwall. Mr Ramsay was a portrait of Leslie Stephen, Mrs Ramsay of their mother, and 'James' of their brother Adrian. The lighthouse was not in the Hebrides as she pretended, but at Godrevy, across the bay from St Ives. She need not have worried. Vanessa wrote her a long letter of gratitude: 'You have given a portrait of mother which is more like her to me than anything I could have conceived of as possible. It is almost painful to have her so raised from the dead.' The book sold well in England and America, and with the profits, the Woolfs bought their first car, a second-hand Singer, which Virginia never learnt to drive.

Vita's return from the Bakhtiari was followed by two over-night expeditions. She went to Oxford to hear Virginia lecture to undergraduates on Poetry and Fiction, and on 28–9 June 1927, with Harold, Leonard, Quentin and Edward Sack-ville-West, they took the night train to Yorkshire to view the total eclipse of the sun in a cloudy dawn. I have photographs of the occasion. The party looks dismally cold and unbreak-fasted. Virginia wrote in her diary, 'Then it was all over till 1999'. It was startling to find her reaching so far into the future to nominate the very year (in fact the actual day, 11 August 1999, on which I was writing these lines) when to English observers the sun would next be extinguished by the moon. She recalled the whole episode in the final pages of *The Waves*.

VIII

THEN CAME *Orlando*. *Mrs Dalloway* had made Virginia known. *To the Lighthouse* made her well known. *Orlando* made her famous.

She was anxious to start on *The Waves* as soon as she had finished 'Phases of Fiction', which she planned as a short history of English literature, but she put both aside when an idea flashed into her mind. She wrote to Vita:

Yesterday morning I was in despair. ... I couldn't screw a word from me; and at last dropped my head in my hands, dipped my pen in the ink, and wrote these words, as if automatically, on a clean sheet: Orlando: a Biography. No sooner had I done this than my body was flooded with rapture and my brain with ideas. I wrote rapidly till 12. ... But listen: suppose Orlando turns out to be Vita; and it's all about you and the lusts of your flesh and the lure of your mind (heart you have none, who go gallivanting down the lanes with Campbell) ... shall you mind?

Vita did not in the least mind. She was enchanted. But when she came to quote this letter in a broadcast many years after Virginia's death, she omitted the words 'lusts of your flesh' and the reference to Campbell, because the book, although in one sense it was a hymn of gratitude for all the happiness that Vita had given her, in another it was a reproach for deserting her for Mary Campbell, Vita's new lover. Campbell might be younger and more luscious, but Virginia had the better mind. She would recapture Vita by writing a book about her, so ingenious, so affectionate that Vita would be unable to resist its appeal.

Mary Campbell was the wife of the South African poet Roy Campbell. They had come to live in Vita's village, and when she discovered them, she invited them to move into the cottage (*our* cottage, when we were at boarding school), where they could live rent-free and Mary could easily slip down the garden path to the main house where Vita lived. She had fallen deeply in love with Mary. In a single night, when Mary was away, she wrote twelve sonnets to her, some of which the Hogarth Press later published. Roy found out about the affair and was furious. Kitchen knives were brandished. Then he threatened to commit suicide. Vita rushed to Virginia and sobbed her heart out. *Orlando* was one result.

There were other family links. Harold Nicolson had just published *Some People*, a collection of stories which he had written during lonely evenings in Teheran, developing a new form of fiction, half true, half fantasy, in which real people like Harold himself were put in imaginary situations, and imaginary people in real situations. Virginia was impressed by Harold's book: he was not as stupid as she once thought. She reviewed it in the *New York Herald Tribune* under the heading, 'The New Biography', and something of its manner crept into *Orlando*, elaborating his fact-cum-fiction into an elegant arabesque. She would turn Orlando from man into woman halfway through the book, to suggest that human nature, especially Vita's, is androgynous, 'that a woman could be as tolerant and free-spoken as a man, and a man as strange and subtle as a woman', as she expressed it in the book itself. Orlando does not change her nature when she changes sex. All the time she is curiously like Vanessa – competent, audacious, stand-offish, often tongue-tied. Virginia also determined to identify Vita with Knole for ever, in compensation for losing it. In January 1928, when Virginia was writing the book, Vita's father, Lord Sackville, died, and it turned into a memorial mass for him and for Vita's double loss. As a girl, his only child, she could not inherit the house, which she had loved as profoundly as she had loved her father. It passed, with the Sackville title, to her uncle Charles. *Orlando* would be her consolation. It had turned into something much more than the joke Virginia had first intended.

There was another ingredient to this complex story. Virginia used it as a medium to explore English history and literature. Therefore it must extend over several centuries, beginning with Vita (as a boy) in the reign of Queen Elizabeth I and ending with Vita (as a woman) in 1928, the year of publication. She ages twenty years in 350. Virginia did not intend her history or her geography to be taken seriously. St Paul's Cathedral is given a dome before the Great Fire of London destroyed its spire; there is no mention whatever of vast events like the Civil War or the American Revolution; the mountains of Wales are visible from the park at Knole. But she made no attempt to conceal the identity of her central character. The book was dedicated to Vita; it contained photographs of her in different guises; and it is full of sly allusions to their personal lives. Orlando drives a four-in-hand as boldly as in real life Vita drove a Ford; Violet Trefusis is reincarnated as a Russian princess, and they meet at the ice carnival on the Thames in 1608 (a scene brilliantly imagined by Sally Potter in her film of the book in 1993); Vita's rejected lover, Lord Lascelles, becomes inexplicably the Archduchess Harriet; and she discovers Shakespeare sitting with a tankard of beer and a pen in his hands, in the servants' hall at Knole.

It is a fantasy. It is Vita-in-Wonderland. It is an impressionist picture – you must stand back from it to grasp its meaning. But it was rooted in Knole, where the manuscript is now on public display. While Virginia was writing it, my brother and I went with her more than once to pace the long galleries, and she would ask us, pointing at a picture, 'Who's that? What was she like?', and as we never knew, she would invent a name and a character on the spot, so that we came to guess something of her intention. Nobody, not even Vita, read a word of it until it was in print. Even when they spent a week together in Burgundy shortly before publication, they scarcely mentioned it. Then, on 11 October 1928 (which are also the last words of the book), Vita received her specially bound copy. She was almost incoherent with astonishment and delight. *Orlando* celebrated their love-affair – and defused it.

IX

WHILE THE BOOK was still simmering in the literary journals, they went to Cambridge together. Virginia was giving at Girton College the second of two lectures which she turned into *A Room of One's Own*. It was overtly feminist, and it became for a time, specially for Americans, the bible of the feminist movement. It stated the case with overwhelming force, grace and humour. Since the book originated as lectures, its style was conversational, more like her letters than her diary. As Quentin Bell said of it, 'In *A Room* one can hear her speaking. In her novels she is thinking'. But, strangely, he thought her tone too mild, too conciliatory, while to me it is fierce beyond reasonableness. She upbraids the male sex for their love of war and making money. She dwells on the disadvantages that women have endured, particularly as writers. They did not have a chance. If Shakespeare had had an equally brilliant sister, not a word of what she wrote would have survived – if she had been allowed by her parents or husband to write any words at all. Even Jane Austen was obliged to hide her manuscripts from prying eyes: 'There was something discreditable in writing *Pride and Prejudice*', Virginia said, ignoring the fact that Jane's father had urged her to publish it. If she covered up her manuscript when someone entered the room, so did Virginia, because until a book is published, it is the most intimate of secrets. Was it really necessary for a woman to have a room of her own before she could write a line? Virginia herself chose the busy stockroom in Tavistock Square, when the upper floors of the house contained several rooms where she could have found peace. Her claim that in the nineteenth century women of genius were stifled by men sits oddly beside the achievements of Austen, the Brontës, Gaskell and George Eliot, and even in Shakespeare's day they were not hammered into insignificance, if we take Portia, Olivia and Desdemona as representatives of contemporary women of mettle.

A Room of One's Own was in part a polemic, in part a fantasy. The mood of *Orlando* was still upon her. She was having fun, but the fun was soured by a note of real bitterness. 'Why did men drink wine and women water?', she asked again. In Bloomsbury both sexes drank wine. And was not Virginia herself, by her conduct and achievements, proof that women of her class were already emancipated? She was not thinking of classes other than her own. Among her friends, only Ethel Smyth considered that her career had been thwarted by masculine presumption. When, a few years later, Virginia wrote an introduction to a collection of reminiscences by working women (*Life As We Have Known It*), she was appalled by their conventionality. They thought it vulgar for a woman to smoke a pipe or read detective novels. 'I don't think they will be poets or novelists for another hundred years or so', she told Margaret Llewellyn-Davies.

Vita was at a loss how to deal with the book in one of her broadcasts on current literature, for she disliked its stridency as much as she disliked *Three Guineas* ten years later for the same reason. She commended *A Room* to her listeners for its 'common sense', when common sense was the last quality that Virginia had envisaged. It was not her style. What can Vita have thought, sitting in the lecture hall at Girton, when she heard Virginia declare, 'Women have had less intellectual freedom than the sons of Athenian slaves', as if there had been no improvement since then, no Acts of Parliament giving women political equality with men, and, for that matter, no Girton? She made great play, in the most famous passage of the book, with the contrast between men's and women's colleges. At King's she had lunched superbly off sole, partridge and a sugary confection, flavoured with red wine and white. At Newnham (another women's college) the menu for supper was soup, beef, prunes and custard, and for drink, 'the water-jug was liberally passed round'. How could conversation flourish, how could genius take root, on such a diet? She did not mention that the lunch was given in his own rooms at King's by one of the Fellows, George Rylands, and at Newnham the supper was in hall with the students. It was undergraduate fare.

Two incidents occurred at this time to test Virginia's beliefs. First there was *The Well of Loneliness*, a novel by Radclyffe Hall which dealt openly with the subject of lesbianism. As soon as it was published, the press attacked it for indecency. The editor of the *Sunday Express* wrote, 'I would rather give a healthy boy or a healthy girl a phial of prussic acid than this novel'. The publisher, Jonathan Cape, voluntarily submitted it to the judgment of the Home Secretary, who declared it obscene, and it was withdrawn from circulation. This act of censorship aroused the fury of Bloomsbury, although their common opinion was that the book was bad and its author conceited. E.M. Forster took the lead in organizing a petition to reverse the Home Secretary's ban, and persuaded Virginia to sign a letter to the *Nation* pleading that, although lesbianism was 'uninteresting and repellent to the majority', it was a fact of life and therefore a legitimate subject for literature. Forster was himself homosexual, but during a visit to the Woolfs in Sussex he declared, according to Virginia's diary, that 'he thought Sapphism disgusting: partly from convention, partly because he disliked that women should be independent of men'. She seems to have taken this provocative statement calmly. She continued to support Forster and Hall, and offered to give evidence, presumably of literary merit, on behalf of the book, though Leonard advised her not to become personally involved, in case she came to be regarded as a mouthpiece for lesbianism and blacken the fair name of Bloomsbury. She persisted, attending the court with a galaxy of other intellectuals, but their claim that *The Well of Loneliness* was a serious work of art was declared irrelevant by the magistrate, and the novel remained on the index of banned books till 1949.

Virginia had done her best for a woman-writer whom she did not much like. Then another situation arose which concerned her more personally. Vita had acquired a new lover after Mary Campbell. She was Hilda Matheson, talks director of the BBC. They had gone on a walking tour in France, and Virginia was openly jealous, accusing Vita, with some justice, of having concealed this holiday from her. It was not simply that Hilda seemed to have supplanted her: Virginia disliked her for other reasons. She was a woman of real ability and determination. She had gained a high position in the BBC, and had persuaded eminent men and women, including Wells and Shaw, to broadcast on subjects of their own choice. Virginia herself had contributed to a discussion with Leonard, but the experience only added to her dislike of Hilda. She had never met a woman like her before. She thought her pushing. 'Her earnest aspiring competent wooden face appears before me,' she wrote in her diary. 'A queer trait in Vita – a passion for the earnest middle-class intellectual, however drab and dreary.' This description of Hilda was unfair. She fought valiantly for high standards in broadcasting which are still valid today. As her biographer, Michael Carney, has written, 'She was a genuine creative spirit, an administrator and programme-maker of genius'. But Virginia could not bring herself to admire an ambitious woman who fought her corner in a man's world. She had as instinctive a dislike for organizing women as she had for organizing men. She told Vita that Hilda 'affects me as a strong purge, as a hair-shirt, as a foggy day, as a cold in the head'. When Hilda Matheson died in 1940, she was still unreconciled: 'I didn't get on with her: she seemed so dried, so official', but that was not true of Hilda, whom I had come to know well and love.

The Matheson affair marked a decline in the Virginia–Vita relationship. They remained friends until Virginia's death, and in the early years of World War II something of their early intimacy revived. But when in January 1929 they met in Berlin, where Harold was now Counsellor in the British Embassy, the visit was a failure. Leonard refused to attend a lunch party of German politicians which Harold had arranged in his honour, and Virginia, hating Berlin and the trappings of diplomacy as much as Vita did, was miserable. One day, when they lunched alone together, Virginia attempted to restore their old relationship only to be met with unexpected coolness. Then there was an incident that involved myself. The party, which included Vanessa and Duncan, went to a controversial film titled *Sturm über Asien*, and I, aged eleven, was refused admission. Vita was enraged by this display of pre-Hitler puritanism, and took me back to my father's flat through snow-slushed streets. I remember the gloom of the occasion, the anger, the incompatibility, which Vanessa's contempt for Vita's distress did nothing to allay.

Virginia returned from Berlin in a state of collapse, due partly to the 'rackety' life she had endured there, and partly to a pill which upset her more than the seasickness it was intended to cure. She was bedridden for a month. Her main correspondent was still Vita ('Have you any love for me, or only the appreciation which one member of the PEN has for another?'), and when she recovered, her time was occupied by two major novels, Vita's *The Edwardians*, which the Hogarth Press published, and her own masterpiece, *The Waves*.

The Edwardians, like *Orlando*, was about Knole and the Sackville family. It was a romantic story – and Vita could tell a story well – in which she tried to reconcile her love of tradition with her conviction that the values of Edwardian society were false. It was a best-seller, the choice of the Book Societies both in Britain and America, and the Hogarth Press, with its wholly inadequate staff, handled the rush of business with success, as they did with Vita's next book, *All Passion Spent*, which was also a best-seller. It was Vita's finest novel, the reflections of an old woman, Lady Slane, on how convention had denied her any freedom of action or expression.

Virginia liked it more than *The Edwardians*, and was impressed by Vita's declaration that she didn't care a scrap for her novels. She wished to be remembered as a poet. She wrote fiction only in order to pay the school bills for Ben and me. She had written them at speed.

The Waves, on the other hand, was the product of intense thought and labour. It was so original a book that only a few grasped its purpose. In outline, it was the outcome ('story' is not a word that one can use in this connection) of six friends soliloquizing about their lives from childhood to middle age. Their individual contributions were separated by lyrical passages describing the rising and setting of the sun over the sea. When she began it in 1929, she told her nephew Quentin that it was to be 'an entirely new kind of book', and when it was published in 1931, she replied to an ecstatic letter from Goldsworthy Lowes Dickinson, 'I did mean that in some vague way we are the same person, and not separate people. The six characters are supposed to be one.' This gives an indication of the complexity of the book. It was a rainbow of different colours forming a single arc, the most poetic of her novels. It made every reader feel inadequate. Yet it sold 6,500 copies in three weeks.

Never had she concentrated so hard over a book. The history of its composition is amazing. She wrote it in manuscript twice over, the second version bearing little relation to the first. We can follow its progress in her diary. It began to torment her. 'I write variations of every sentence; compromises; bad shots; possibilities. . . . I wish I enjoyed it more.' She fell ill, but the book continued to ferment like wine in the cask. Each afternoon she typed out what she had written in the morning, altering as she went, and then she had it retyped professionally, and further revised it, then again slightly in proof. 'Never', she wrote, 'have I screwed my brain so tight over a book.' She barely mentioned the struggle in her letters. It was an intensely private labour, the printed book the only public declaration of her intent. Years later she wrote to Edward Sackville-West, 'It's the only one of my books that I can sometimes read with pleasure. Not that I wrote it with pleasure, but in a kind of trance into which I suppose I shall never sink again.'

Her distractions were many, because except when she was ill, she never relaxed for a moment her busy social life, her manifold correspondence, or her work for the Hogarth Press reading innumerable manuscripts and 'travelling' their books with Leonard to the West Country as far as Penzance. There is something touching about the picture of these two middle-aged intellectuals trying to persuade indifferent, and some-times downright insulting, booksellers to take their highbrow publications. 'It's becoming too much', Virginia confessed to Vanessa. But instead of giving up, they enlisted John Lehmann as manager, with the intention of making him a partner after an eight-month trial. He was much more than a manager. He brought them young authors like Stephen Spender, W.H. Auden and Cecil Day-Lewis.

Another person entered Virginia's life contemporary with her writing of *The Waves*, who to some extent took Vita's place as her confidante and correspondent-in-chief for the next ten years, but without reciprocated love. Although Ethel Smyth undoubtedly loved Virginia with a sick passion, Virginia tolerated her, rather as she tolerated the Hogarth Press, as a diversion, and then a burden which she could not easily shake off. They had many friends in common, Vita among them, and each had long been interested in the other's books. It was *A Room of One's Own* which compelled Ethel to seek a meeting, since Virginia had expressed precisely the grievance that Ethel had nursed for three decades, the unequal struggle of women artists to win recognition in a man's world. Ethel, now seventy-three years old, was a composer who imagined that only male prejudice had prevented the performance of her works, when in fact it was the other way round. A woman composer was so rare that her very existence excited wonder, and a woman who had added to her reputation in many other ways – by her autobiographies, her friends in high places, her two-month imprisonment as a suffragette – was regarded as a national phenomenon, and her music, like her opera *The Wreckers*, was performed not only because it was fresh and vigorous, but because it was by Ethel Smyth.

Her pursuit of Virginia soon ran into trouble. 'It is like being caught by a giant crab', she complained to Quentin, but Ethel's persistence paid off. This is how I described their relationship in the Introduction to the fourth volume of Virginia's letters, of which 130 were written to Ethel herself:

Virginia was half-amused, half-defensive, referring to 'this curious unnatural friendship', fearing ridicule, fearing too deep an involvement. She was wary of her. They had both voyaged too far before berthing in the same dock. Ethel took the initiative with a volley of questions to which she seldom awaited the replies even if she could hear them [she was very deaf] but they could be repeated in Virginia's letters. Reading them, one hears their talk, the gradual unloading of all that cargo, more reticent on Virginia's side than on Ethel's, but gradually, under pressure, she yielded, and wrote to Ethel about matters that hitherto she had scarcely mentioned to anyone – her madness ['It's terrific, I can assure you'], her feelings about sex ['I was always cowardly'] and even her thoughts of suicide that she had confessed to Leonard ['If you weren't here, I would kill myself']. She began to teach Ethel the benefits of patience and humility, and Ethel became a little calmer, a little less prone to beat the cymbals. Virginia enjoyed the combat, admired her, respected her. She was a gadfly, and paradoxically a solace.

I just remember Ethel. She often came to Long Barn, dressed like a coachman in cloak and tricorn hat, and she was vigorous in a way that didn't frighten children, bursting through the weeks like paper hoops, a woman whose pertinacity was irresistible. Deafness, which can make people tedious to their friends, was for Ethel an asset. She told us to yell at her, and we yelled with an exuberance unequalled when talking to normal people. Once she insisted, when sitting on our terrace at Long Barn, on hearing a nightingale. A bird sang its heart out in the garden, but not a note penetrated to Ethel until it obligingly perched on the table in front of her and gave her a solo performance. How we cheered! How we adored her!

X

IN THE EARLY 1930s the Woolfs went on annual holidays abroad. Now that Virginia's books were earning a higher income, they could afford to travel, and there was always the lure of Vanessa who spent much of the year with Duncan and her children at Cassis in the south of France. They often went further afield, Leonard driving their brand-new Lanchester car over the almost empty roads of France. He wrote that Virginia had a passion for travelling, 'a mixture of exhilaration and relaxation', which refreshed her mind with new sights, sounds and smells. She tolerated discomfort, and was never impatient for quicker progress. It was the journey, not the arrival, that mattered, the slower the better. There were stepping-stones on which they could pause awhile – Montaigne's tower, Joan of Arc's castle – but they rarely visited a museum and scarcely spoke to anyone but servants in the inns, because Virginia was uncertain of her French, and there was no need.

She enjoyed most the countryside and life of the small towns, the scenes that Baedeker leaves out, the smell of aromatic plants on low hills, 'where no one has ever been before', picnicking under cypresses and olive trees, and always the delicious release from London, the joy of being unavailable.

Her excellence as a traveller is best displayed in the letters and diaries she wrote on a tour of Greece in April 1932. She and Leonard were accompanied by Roger Fry and his sister Margery, the one an authority on classical and Byzantine art,

Ethel Smyth in about 1930, when she first came to know Virginia, who was 'half-amused, half-defensive, referring to "this curious unnatural friendship"... But she enjoyed the combat, admired her, respected her. She was a gadfly, and paradoxically a solace.'

the other on the wild flowers. For Virginia it was her second visit. A quarter of a century earlier she had toured many of the same sites – Athens, Nauplia, Mycenae, Corinth – and Greece was little changed. The country roads were so abominable, often as pitted as torrent beds, that few tourists ventured far from Athens. The emptiness of the mountains and the coast gave Virginia infinite delight. It was like Chaucer's England, she said, even Homer's Greece. Her letters and her diary (hardly a phrase repeated from one into the other) were not about the temples and the churches, but about the country and its people. In the diary she made verbal notes, much as a painter might sketch a scene from which to make a finished picture in his studio ('how lovely the pure lip of the sea touching a wild shore, with hills behind, and green plains and red rocks'), but in her letters she took flight, fitting words to images with unequalled virtuosity. To Vita: 'We saw the Greek shepherds' huts in a wood near Marathon, and a lovely dark-olive, red-lipped, pink-shawled girl wandering and spinning thread from a lump of wool.' To Vanessa: 'If ever I had a turn towards Sapphism, it would be revived by the carts of young peasant women in lemon, red and blue handkerchiefs, and the donkeys and the kids and the general fecundity and bareness; and the sea; and the cypresses.' To Ottoline Morrell: 'Not a bungalow, not a kennel, not a teashop. Pure sea water on pure sand is almost the loveliest thing in the world.' It was a lesson in how to travel, how to observe, and how to describe what you observe, as different from the style of her novels as a Cotman is from a Cézanne. She called it the best holiday of her life, and one reason was that it was arduous. She was blistered by the sun and exhausted by the roads, but her endurance was rewarded by the remoteness of the places they visited. She was moved by their stark simplicity. 'I could love Greece as an old woman [she was only fifty] as I once loved Cornwall as a child.'

Another spring holiday, in 1935, was of a very different nature. They drove through Holland, Germany and Austria to Florence and Rome. Leonard had been warned by the Foreign Office that it was inadvisable for a Jew to visit Germany, and they found every town placarded with anti-Semitic posters. But nowhere were they molested, although in the neighbourhood of Bonn they coincided with a visit to the city by Goering, and security was very tight. What might have been ominous attention by the Stormtroopers to Leonard's unmistakable Hebraic features was diverted by Mitz, his marmoset, who was travelling with them. I remember Mitz. The Woolfs brought him to lunch at Sissinghurst, the house to which we had recently moved from Long Barn, and my father, who had a horror of rodents, was amazed that Leonard could endure the pawing of this rat-like creature round his face and neck. Mitz ruined our lunch party. But the Germans adored him, and they were waved through every barrier with blessings and applause.

Virginia never travelled outside western and southern Europe, apart from her two short visits to northern Turkey before her marriage. Her only interest in the Far East was prompted by Arthur Waley's translations from the Chinese. She never visited any part of Africa, never flew in an aeroplane, and never crossed the Atlantic. Although she had two or three invitations to visit America, she never did. She remained as prejudiced against the United States as she would have been against Liberia. Three of her friends were born Americans, Tom Eliot, Logan Pearsall Smith and Ethel Sands, but she counted them as British, unless she was cross with them, when they became Americans again, with all the failings that she associated with that race. 'So ugly, so dusty, so dull', she wrote of two visitors from San Francisco whom she was about to meet for the first time, and when she was introduced to Blanche Knopf, the publisher, all that she could subsequently remember about her were her eyebrows, 'picked out so that one pencil of hair remains in the middle of her forehead: the effect is one of perpetual surprise, and to me unpleasing'. May Sarton, the poet and novelist, was 'that goose – a pale, pretty Shelley-imitation American girl'. New York meant little more to her than the address of her publisher, Harcourt Brace, and the magazines *Vogue* and *Harper's Bazaar*, the generosity of whose cheques she much appreciated. Yale University was only the *Yale Review*, which in 1932 published her *Letter to a Young Poet*, but outside the northeast coast she had little conception what America was really like. When in 1933 Vita and Harold went on a lecture tour of the United States, Virginia wrote to her:

> I imagine you sitting on a tight plush seat in a car, with views of the Middle West – an unattractive land, largely sprinkled with old tin kettles – racing across vast slabs of plate glass. The negroes are spitting in the carriage next door, and after 25 more hours, the train will stop at a town like Peacehaven, only 75 times larger, called Balmoralville, where you will get out, and after a brief snack off clams and iced pear-drops with the Mayor, who is called, I should think, Cyrus K. Hinks, you will go to a large Baptist hall and deliver a lecture on Rimbaud.

Her vision of California was equally fantastic. Writing to

Hugh Walpole, who was in Hollywood, she imagined: 'You are sitting with vast blue plains rolling round you: a virgin forest at your back; a marble city gleaming at your feet; and people so new, so brave, so beautiful and utterly uncontaminated by civilisation, popping in and out of booths and theatres with pistols in their hands and aeroplanes soaring over their heads.' It was as if she considered that an ancient place like Greece must be more virtuous, more estimable, because of its antiquity, than America, which must be brash, unlovable and deficient in all the qualities that she held most dear, just because it was new. She allowed their people no worthwhile literature, no physical evidence of a long tradition, because all these desirable attributes can only be acquired by centuries of effort and suffering. She could fancy herself living in Tuscany, the Dordogne, the Morea, but not conceivably in Maine. It lacked Bloomsbury's patina.

She told an American student who was writing a thesis about her that the name 'Bloomsbury Group ' was 'merely a journalistic phrase which had no meaning', and that was becoming increasingly true. Bloomsbury was unravelling. Vanessa considered that it had died with the outbreak of the First World War. Its membership bifurcated, like a river approaching its delta. They now had different careers, different lovers. Keynes was a senior economist, Duncan Grant and Vanessa fashionable painters and decorators, Roger Fry Slade Professor at Cambridge, Desmond MacCarthy the leading literary critic of his day, Eliot Professor of Poetry at Harvard, Strachey a best-seller, Virginia a genius. Moreover, the Bloomsbury attitudes that had once made them notorious had become commonplace. Women had votes and entered the professions; homosexual love and sex before marriage were tolerated if not yet condoned; censorship of literature was thought old-fashioned; socialism was practised; the League of Nations existed; the Impressionists were accepted, and Diaghilev was the rage. In fact, as Quentin Bell observed in his book about Bloomsbury, 'the audacities of one age became the platitudes of the next'. Only their pacifism was not in general found acceptable, and Bloomsbury itself was fast abandoning it as a creed.

They did not correspond or meet as regularly as in the past, but there was still the Memoir Club, and odd meals and visits which reunited individuals for an hour or a day. Monk's House, for all its discomforts, was a favourite resort, and it was at Charleston that Strachey read aloud the first chapters of *Eminent Victorians* and Keynes composed his *Economic Consequences of the Peace* before he moved with his wife to Tilton House, only half a mile away. For Virginia these friendships formed the core of her life. When Lytton died of stomach cancer in 1932, aged only fifty-two, she wrote to Ottoline, 'I have got a queer feeling that I'm hearing him talk in the next room – the talk I always want to go on with. I have a million things to tell him, and never shall.' His death was followed within a few weeks by Carrington's suicide. She thought life unbearable without him. The day after Leonard and Virginia had visited her at Ham Spray, she borrowed a rifle, ostensibly to shoot rabbits, and shot herself. She took six hours to die. Leonard thought her act histrionic, but later generations have come to regard her death as Bloomsbury's finest gesture, a symbol of their incandescent gift for friendship. Then Roger Fry died, in 1934, two years after his journey to Greece with the Woolfs, and Virginia wrote of him in her diary, 'Dignified and honest and large – something ripe and musical about him – and then the fun, and the fact that he had lived with such variety and generosity and curiosity'. She called him 'the most intelligent of my friends, profusely, ridiculously, perpetually creative'.

She had diversions to console her for these losses, and some new pleasures – a camera, an inflatable canoe in which she paddled down the Ouse, another pool for Leonard's garden, a Frigidaire for Monk's kitchen, Orlando's new bedroom for herself, learning Italian once more. The literary world wondered what she would write next. Would *The Waves* be followed by another novel in the same elusive style? She published several essays in a second series of *The Common Reader*, and then surprised everyone by writing a short novel about a dog. *Flush* was the title of the book and the name of the dog, which had belonged to Elizabeth Barrett Browning. No topic is more prone to sentimentality than dog and cat stories. People remembered *Where's Master?*, a best-selling novel, ostensibly written by Caesar, Edward VII's dog, which had followed the King's coffin to the grave. Virginia's book never pretended that Flush could talk or even think like a human being: but he could observe, and Mrs Browning would do the talking for him. The book was poetic. Through Flush's eyes she retold the story of Elizabeth's elopement with Robert Browning. It was the only work of which Virginia gave me a copy, possibly because it was the only one which a child could be expected to understand. She was not pleased with it. She had started it 'to let my brain cool' after *The Waves*. It was 'easy indolent writing'. But as she finished her 30,000 words, she regretted the time she had spent writing them. She told Vita that it was 'a foolish, witless joke', and herself that it was 'silly', at one moment too slight, at the next too serious. Nevertheless, it was a great success, the Book Society choice in England and America. Virginia despised the critics who praised it and the public who bought it, but when Rebecca West called it 'a family joke', she was upset, because she agreed. Her mind was on something larger, *The Pargiters*, which came to birth four years later as *The Years*.

Her fame was becoming more of a disability than a reward. It meant constant interruptions – letters from strangers, requests for interviews, photographs, autographs, the tedium, as she expressed it, of 'seeing and being seen'. She did not resent visits from friends old and new (Elizabeth Bowen, William Plomer) who understood a writer's need for solitude, so much as visits from friends of friends who did not. Even Peter Quennell, a poet, critic and biographer of intelligence and merit, was lambasted by Virginia as 'a pushing and at the same time wriggling eel', just because the Woolfs were landed with him as a weekend guest. When Ethel Smyth begged her to come to Woking and meet some of Ethel's neighbours, Virginia turned on her with a machine-gun. How could Ethel imagine for a moment that she had time to spare for 'admirers', that she was flattered by the invitation? 'You've been thinking I'm that sort of person – that's how I spend my time, in a rose-coloured teagown, signing autographs.'

Ethel was capable of rallying from a snub in a way that Vita never could, and continued to exert a pressure to which Virginia unexpectedly succumbed, for she was fond of Ethel, and admired her pertinacity even when she was the victim of it. Vita, shyer, more reticent in public, and reluctant to intrude on Virginia's privacy now that she had lost her love, withdrew to Sissinghurst, cultivated her garden, and moved into a new phase of her life, reflecting on the nature of religion, as her poems *Solitude* and *Sissinghurst* (the latter dedicated to Virginia) excellently reveal. They were followed by her biographies of Joan of Arc and St Teresa of Avila. Virginia came three or four times to Sissinghurst with Leonard, but spent only a single night there, in Harold's bedroom when he was away. Her affection for Vita was summed up in a phrase: 'I can't deny that I have a sort of dying ember in my heart for you.'

Virginia was indifferent to honours. She had accepted the Femina Prize for *To the Lighthouse*, possibly because she was then relatively unknown. But now that her name was widely canvassed as the protagonist of a new type of fiction, public tributes were thrust upon her and she refused them all. She would not accept from the Crown the Companion of Honour (which Vita did accept for herself), the most enviable award for the arts after the Order of Merit. She refused an honorary degree from Manchester University, writing to the Vice-Chancellor a letter that started, 'I need not say how deeply I am honoured . . .', but in her diary she described it as 'all that humbug'. More surprising was her refusal to give the Clark Lectures at Cambridge. It was a highly prestigious invitation. Her own father had given the first lectures in 1883, and Virginia was the first woman to be invited to succeed him. Would it not advance the cause of women to accept? But no. Her formal reason for declining was that she had no time: it would take at least a year to prepare the six lectures, and she was anxious to make progress with her novel. But her private reasons were that she considered university lectures 'an obsolete practice inherited from the Middle Ages when books were scarce. Students should read, not listen. To swallow instruction from a lectern is like sipping English literature through a straw. Lectures, she was to proclaim in *Three Guineas*, only pander to the vanity of the lecturer and stimulate conflict between academics. What's more, there would probably be a reception after each lecture. Sherry and cocktails would be served, which seemed to her even less palatable than the prunes and custard at Newnham. 'It is a vain and vicious system', she declared, but she knew that to utter such heresies at Cambridge would be an intolerable breach of manners. So she refused.

When Walter Sickert asked her to write about his paintings, she consented with misgivings. She was no art critic. Her letters to Vanessa on the subject were full of love and admiration, as were Vanessa's to her about her novels, but each was wary of the other, fearing to write something inadvertently wounding or foolish. In criticizing the Pre-Raphaelites, companions of her father, Virginia was outspokenly hostile. On an exhibition of Edward Burne-Jones's paintings, she wrote, 'The suavity, the sinuosity, the way the private parts are merely clouded – it's all a romantic dream, which makes me think of Hyde Park Gate.' With Sickert it was a different matter. She had genuinely admired his pictures, but when she met him face to face, she was put off by his vanity and weariness, 'his hard little eyes, very old [he was seventy-three], no illusion about his own greatness'. Still, she was committed, and urged by Vanessa, she wrote a brilliant essay comparing portraiture to biography, and coming to the conclusion that painting was the more truthful, although 'we cannot penetrate the zone of silence in the middle of every art'. Sickert was delighted. He told her that it was the only criticism of his work worth having. Not surprisingly, said Virginia to herself, as she had praised him throughout. Fry's and Clive's verdicts on her essay were more astringent.

It is an example of Virginia's courtesy and kindness. Although her letters often crossed the borderline, they pricked more than gashed. It was the custom of Bloomsbury to tease. They were all guilty of ridiculing each other. But if someone were in serious trouble, or unlikely to respond to teasing with the tolerance of Ethel Smyth, Virginia would be endearingly sympathetic. An instance is her reply to an American, John Nef, who sent her his two-volume work *The Rise of the British Coal Industry*. Instead of answering that she greatly looked forward to reading it (the formula recommended by Harold Macmillan, the statesman-publisher), she read it, and thanked him for his 'delightful present. .... I am enjoying your coal much more than all the manuscripts which I should be reading'. The deceit (if it was one) was legitimate. But with her intimates there was no need. She could scold, but more often she encouraged, particularly Vanessa's children. She sat through Angelica's interminable school play; she applauded Julian for writing a dissertation on 'The Good' in the hope of a Fellowship at King's College, Cambridge; and with Quentin she carried on a merry type-written correspondence, the speed of her typing keeping pace with the cataract of her ideas.

There was still the problem of being over-visited. Typical of her despair and the humour with which she controlled it was this letter to Ethel Smyth:

Tom Eliot for twenty-four hours solid talk yesterday; Rosamond Lehmann now coming for lunch; Oliver Strachey, tea; Lady Colefax I have refused; must go to London to write about 12th Night. Must write journalism. Must see friends. Have therefore decided from today to give up all other writing in order to see there's beef for lunch and cakes for tea. Am going to spend all my money on clothes, face powder. . . . Fingers to be red. Toes to be silver. Face to be lifted, nose to be filled with wax. [Signed] V., who gave up literature at the command of her friends.

There can be no doubt that she resented interruptions, but she spent hours describing them for her friends, perhaps as a warning to them, perhaps as a diversion, more likely as a conductor for her wrath. 'I like it when people actually come, but I love it when they go', was the most charitable of her complaints.

It was untypical of her to wail in public. But she wrote to the *New Statesman* a letter which might have been written today on behalf of all celebrities:

Open the dailies and the weeklies. Among the pictures of Atlantic flyers and murderers you will find portraits of well-known people, and by no means all of them public people, but private people, musicians, writers, painters, artists of all kinds. Their homes are photographed, their families, their gardens, their studios, their bedrooms and their writing-tables. Interviews appear: their opinions on every sort of subject are broadcast.

She admitted that the celebrities often succumbed to this treatment out of kindness to a friend. Can she have been so innocent as to imagine that they all disliked it? Ethel, for one, revelled in public attention. Fame is desirable for those without it, not always detestable to those with it. Virginia was quite capable of mocking her own modesty. At the height of her fame she read a paper to the Memoir Club entitled, 'Am

I a Snob?'. She confessed that Society fascinated her. She would leave a coroneted letter on top of the pile in the hope that visitors would notice it. She cultivated the aristocracy because they behaved 'more naturally' than most people, and she knew that they cultivated her because she was famous. Lady Oxford (Margot Asquith) asked her to write her obituary for *The Times* because 'you are the greatest female writer living'. She did not expect such people to test her intellectually: that was Bloomsbury's function. 'If you ask me would I rather meet Einstein or the Prince of Wales', she wrote in her Memoir, 'I plump for the Prince without hesitation.' The type of person she most disliked were climbers. The snobs who look up are even worse than the snobs who look down. As she was neither, she decided that she was not a snob at all. She was simply curious. She liked nailing people down as specimens, like butterflies. Stephen Spender, aged twenty-four, 'is a nice poetic youth, big-nosed, bright-eyed, like a giant thrush'. Noël Coward 'called me darling, and gave me his glass to drink out of'. Then she would turn suddenly fierce, as when defending Strachey against a man who had called him heartless, 'Lytton had more love in his little finger than that castrated cat in the whole of his mangy stringy partless gutless tailless body.' She knew how to be formidable when she chose.

An excellent example of her reaction to new people and new places is provided by her visit to Ireland in 1934 to stay with Elizabeth Bowen. Virginia had first met her with Lady Ottoline two years before, and did not immediately take to her. She was awkward, she stammered, and was married to the Education Officer for the City of Oxford, Alan Cameron, which was no commendation to Virginia who distrusted officials of all kinds; and she suspected that Elizabeth had modelled her novels on her own. Later, her attitude changed. After the Camerons had moved from Oxford to London, Elizabeth became her literary confidante. Virginia liked *The House in Paris* (1935) very much indeed, and told her so. It was the start of Virginia's most successful literary friendship. Unlike Katherine Mansfield, Elizabeth provoked no jealousy. And unlike Ethel Smyth, she was neither exclamatory nor an intruder.

It was the Woolfs' first visit to Ireland, and their curiosity to see the country was greater than their curiosity to see the Camerons, with whom they stayed but a single night. Virginia disliked their house, Bowen's Court. She called it 'pompous and pretentious and imitative and ruined – a great barrack of grey stone, four storeys and basements, like a town-house, high empty rooms'. That was the verdict she entrusted to her diary. In writing to Vanessa she went further: 'It's a great stone box, but full of Italian mantelpieces and decayed 18th-century furniture, and carpets all in holes. However, they insisted on keeping up a ramshackle kind of state, dressing for dinner and so on.' Worst of all, they found as fellow-guests Cyril Connolly and his wife, to whom Virginia took an instant dislike: 'A less appetising pair I have never seen out of the zoo'. The house and the company had such a depressing effect on her that she descended to ridicule in order to brighten the conversation. According to Connolly's account of their miserable evening, 'she asked Elizabeth Bowen what "unnatural vice" was, and what acts constituted it, and I sensed that she was a virginal and shy character', when she was neither.

On escaping from Bowen's Court they travelled quite extensively through Ireland, and Virginia was entranced by the beauty of the country, its emptiness, its simplicity. She thought it a mixture of Greece, Italy and Cornwall, and, as always, considered buying a small house there, but the idea was short-lived: the landscape was suffused in melancholy, and the houses were either ruined mansions or horrid Victorian cottages. She liked the people. They had a genius for talk. 'I can give no notion of the flowing yet formed sentences, the richness and ease of the language. ... Why aren't these people the greatest novelists in the world?'

However, when they reached Dublin, she spared no thought for James Joyce, and unexpectedly did not find the city beautiful, when it is one of the loveliest capitals in Europe. Her taste had never been for urban or Palladian architecture. She thought Dublin's wonderful squares poor replicas of Bloomsbury's, and its population unsettled, feverish. This was not, as one might expect, due to the rise of the Fianna Fáil under de Valera, but to their poverty and lack of spirit – 'no luxury, no creation, no stir, only the dregs of London, rather wishy-washy, as if suburbanised'. 'No', she concluded in her diary, 'it wouldn't do, living in Ireland, in spite of the rocks and the desolate bays. It would lower the pulse of the heart.'

She returned to England with a dose of flu which added to her melancholy, but one should not think of her as normally morose or disapproving. Her usual expression was contemplative, not, like Leonard's, severe, and when she looked up, it was with a smile brimming with new ideas and phrases. She enjoyed provoking people, but not aggressively. As boys we felt ourselves under observation, but not under scrutiny. Her manner was more courteous than polite. By her laughter she would arouse the laughter of other people, and if she did not thrust herself forward in conversation, nor did she shrink. She wanted people to display their best in her company: innkeepers must be welcoming, intellectuals entertaining, children eager. And she would poke at our silences. When we were throwing fragments of bread to the ducks one day, she said, 'How would you describe the noise that the bread makes when it hits the water?' 'Splash?', we suggested. 'No.' 'Splosh?' 'No, no.' 'Then what?' 'Umph', she said. 'But there's no such word!' 'There is now.'

Once I travelled up to London alone with her by train. As we drew out of our local station, she whispered to me:

'You see that man in the corner?'

'Yes.'

'He's a bus conductor from Leeds. He's been on holiday with his uncle, who has a farm near here.'

'But, Virginia, how can you possibly know that? You've never seen him before.'

'No question about it.'

And then she told me, during the whole half-hour that the journey took, the life story of this man, who remained, puffing at his pipe, totally unaware that he was now a figure in twentieth-century literature.

XI

THE WOOLFS CONTINUED to alternate between Monk's House and Tavistock Square, a week or two at a time in each. In the country Virginia would walk the Downs, and cook a little (she baked good bread), and play skilfully with bowls on the lawn. She also took lessons to improve her French, and opened an exhibition of Roger Fry's paintings. She wrote, and she read. Her reading was prodigious. Most authors, when deeply engaged in writing a new book, as she was with *The Pargiters*, rarely give themselves time to read anything not related to it. But Virginia on returning from a long walk would take up *Timon of Athens*, the biography of an eighteenth century parson, *David Copperfield* for the sixth time, or the Bible, for its language, not its doctrine. In addition to the manuscripts submitted to the Hogarth Press, there were books by friends like Ethel Smyth or Stephen Spender, on which she would comment candidly, and usually end with the propitiatory sentence, 'But pay no attention to this', knowing that they always would. She found it difficult to judge contemporaries. They were like people singing in the next room, too loud, too near. 'Hence my unfairness to [D.H.] Lawrence', she wrote. 'How can you put him into the very great? To me he's like an express train running through a tunnel – one shriek, sparks, smoke and gone.' Nor did T.S. Eliot escape her censure. The Woolfs went to a performance of *Murder in the Cathedral*: 'I had almost to carry Leonard out, shrieking.'

For Angelica's birthday in 1935 she staged the only performance of her only play, *Freshwater*, a comedy about Mrs Cameron, the photographer, and her friends in the Isle of Wight. She had first drafted it in 1923, and now wrote a second version, which was performed in Vanessa's studio in Fitzroy Square to an audience of eighty friends. Julia Cameron's role was taken by Vanessa, her husband's by Leonard, and Ellen Terry's by Angelica. Other parts were allotted to Duncan Grant, Adrian Stephen and Julian Bell. Virginia was the producer and prompter.

Further interruptions were caused by political tensions at home and abroad. Hitler was now the German Chancellor, and had murdered some of his closest associates. Mussolini invaded Abyssinia. The Labour Party was split on what attitude to take. Virginia attended, as a reluctant and scornful spectator, its annual conference at Brighton, where the pacifist George Lansbury was squashed by Ernest Bevin, 'like a snake who's swallowed a toad'. She could not bring herself to think that these people or their debates could add an ounce to human happiness, but there was no avoiding them, now that Leonard was deeply involved. Kingsley Martin (editor of the left-wing *New Statesman*) was a constant self-invited guest, and the radio in London and in the country was tuned to every news bulletin. To please Leonard, she canvassed support for an anti-Fascist exhibition, probably unaware that it was Communist-inspired, and even wrote an article for the Marxist *Daily Worker*. But when she was approached to succeed H.G. Wells as President of PEN, the international society of authors which was much concerned with human rights, she exploded: 'I flicked my hand, as a Greek woman flicks a bug off her child's head', she wrote to Ethel. 'Conceive their damned insolence! Ten dinners a year, and I to sit at the head of this puling company of back-scratchers, and administer balm!'

Pinka died, the spaniel immortalized as Flush, but Mitz the marmoset lived on. With Vanessa spending half the year at Cassis, and her son Julian teaching in a remote university in China, it was to those two that Virginia addressed her most entertaining gossip, hopping from twig to twig like Jane Austen in her letters to her sister Cassandra. She resembled a pianist, playing with her right hand the lighter notes (her letters) and with her left the more sombre (her diary), and it is by means of this antiphony that we can follow with unparalleled intimacy the progress of *The Years*. In the letters she described her struggle as if it were little more than an irritating cough that she could not shake off: in her diary, she was a woman in labour.

She had begun the book, when it was called *The Pargiters*, in 1932, and in nine weeks wrote 60,000 words, every one of which she scrapped. She was alternately elated and profoundly depressed. At one moment her brain felt like 'a Rolls Royce engine, purring its 70 miles an hour', and at the next she was writing 'feeble twaddle'. Typical diary entries were: 10 June 1935: 'Working very hard. I think I shall rush these scenes off.' 11 June: 'Yet I cannot write this morning.' 12 September: 'Never have I had such a hot balloon in my head as re-writing *The Years* because it's so long and the pressure is so terrific. But I will use all my art to keep my head sane.' She was fifty-three, the year of her menopause, and Leonard was anxious. In March 1936 she wrote, again in her diary: 'I must very nearly verge on insanity. I think I get so deep in this book I don't know what I am doing. Find myself walking along the Strand talking aloud.' And about the book itself:

'Such twilight gossip, it seemed, such a show-up of my own decrepitude.' Next morning, it seemed not quite so bad: 'On the contrary, a full bustling-like book'. Weeks later, 'I have never suffered, since *The Voyage Out*, such acute despair on re-reading.' In April 1936 Leonard feared that she might suffer a complete mental collapse and took her to Cornwall for a fortnight. Virginia put the proofs aside for two months before starting to correct them, and then she cut out 'enormous chunks', amounting to 250 pages. Even after such drastic surgery, it was still the longest of her books.

So much for her private ordeal. The 'sickle side of the moon' (words that we adapted for the title of the fifth volume of her letters) was her social and family life which she never neglected even when her spirits were lowest. She did not conceal from her friends the suffering that the book caused her, but her hints were self-reproachful, never self-pitying. To Dadie Rylands, 'It is wholly worthless'. To Ethel, 'a hopeless bad book. Verbose, foolish.' To Vanessa, 'this long weary dreary book'. To Ottoline, 'long and dreary'. To Ethel again, 'I don't know or care if it's the worst book or the best'. To Janet Case, 'very bad'. And to Vita. 'I should be delighted to tie a stone to it, and drop it into the Atlantic.'

She was steeling herself to accept the criticism she expected by anticipating it herself. Nobody, surely, could think quite so badly of it as she did. Then came the moment when she must show it to Leonard. As always, he must be her first reader. She relied entirely on his judgement whether to publish the book or scrap it. In her diary for 3 November 1936 she described the scene:

On Sunday I started to read the proofs. When I had read to the end of the first section, I was in despair: stony but convinced despair. I said, This is happily so bad that there can be no question about it. I must carry the proofs, like a dead cat, to Leonard and tell him to burn them unread. This I did. [She then goes for a short walk through Holborn.] I was no longer Virginia, the genius, but only a perfectly insignificant yet content – shall I call it spirit? a body? And very tired, Very old. [Various social engagements intervene]. We went home, and L. read and read and said nothing. I began to feel acutely depressed. . . . Suddenly L. put down his proof and said he thought it extraordinarily good – as good as any of them.

Two days later he finished it. 'L. put down his last sheet about 12 last night, and could not speak. He was in tears. He says it is "a most remarkable book" – he likes it better than *The Waves*, and has not a spark of doubt that it must be published. The moment of relief was divine.'

In fact, Leonard was exaggerating. In one of his autobiographical volumes, *Downhill All the Way*, he confessed: 'I knew that unless I could give a completely favourable verdict, she would be in despair and would have a very serious breakdown. . . . The verdict which I gave her was not absolutely and completely what I thought about it. I praised the book more than I should have done if she had been well.' He does not say why he found it disappointing. His imprimatur was sufficient. She returned to the proofs, revised them extensively once more, and three weeks later was still confident: 'It seems to me to come off at the end. Anyhow to be a taut real strenuous book: with some beauty and poetry too. A full packed book. Feel a little exalted. Nor need I care much what people say.'

The Years was published in March 1937, five years after its conception. The days of waiting were dull, cold torture to her, but all except very few of the reviews were superlative. She was not, as she had expected, ridiculed. On reading Basil de Selincourt's review in *The Observer*, she thought, with delight, of other people reading it. She was not a failure. People would talk about her book, praise it, buy it. She was as happy as a first novelist who buys the *Evening Standard*, opens it in the Underground, and finds her book glowing on an inner page. Then she could be cast down by a single mildly hostile notice like Edwin Muir's in *The Listener*, 'All the lights sank', she wrote on perusing it, 'my reed bent to the ground. Dead and disappointing – so I am found out, and that odious rice-pudding of a book is what I thought it – a dank failure.'

She had been nervous that people would expect another cloudy, lyrical book like *The Waves*, and would be disappointed that the narrative of *The Years* was more conventional, direct. She told Stephen Spender that this time she wanted to catch the attention of the general reader. But nobody could have written *The Years*, as de Selincourt said, who had not already written *The Waves*. Ostensibly it was about a family, the Pargiters, who began in a Victorian house like Hyde Park Gate in the 1880s, and we follow their branching, fraying lives until the year of the book's publication. It is in part autobiographical. We are given a taste of Virginia's experience in the First World War, under bombardment in London, and of the major themes which concerned her, like the subordination of women and her agnosticism. Take this passage describing the funeral of Mrs Pargiter, as her daughter listens to the vicar pronouncing a benediction over the open grave:

'We give thee hearty, thanks', said the voice, 'for that it has pleased thee to deliver this our sister out of the miseries of this sinful world'. 'What a lie!', she cried to herself. 'What a damnable lie!' He had robbed her of the one feeling that was genuine.

That was the defiant Virginia speaking. We also hear Virginia the poet. She, who had never written a line of poetry in her life, could devote an entire page of her novel to rain, not as Hardy would have done it, expositorily, but like Spenser, evocatively. There is a touch of Bloomsbury too. The second-generation Pargiters are unafraid to discuss sex, war, cruelty, the poor, the rich, youth contrasted with age, permanence with change, but they were less adventurous than Bloomsbury. They did not voyage out.

Although it was more clairvoyance than simple narrative, the book was an immediate success with a public who had come to regard Virginia Woolf's novels with the same awe that the next generation paid to Henry Moore's sculptures. In England its sales restored the Woolfs' finances, which, after the long interval since the success of *Flush*, had started to wobble again. In America, as a reward for Donald Brace's infinite patience with Virginia's constant postponements, it sold 25,000 copies in two months, and for weeks remained top of the fiction best-seller list. As Mitchell Leaska, himself an American, has remarked, 'She was left with the grotesque fact that her most certain failure had become her greatest popular success.'

The long process of correcting the proofs of *The Years* coincided with the start of two other major projects in Virginia's literary life – her biography of Roger Fry, which his sisters had begged her to undertake, and her polemic, *Three*

Guineas. She enjoyed the polemic, for which she had begun to collect material, more than the biography, since there was no restriction on what she wanted to say about men and war, but with Fry there were personal problems of discretion: he had been Vanessa's lover; Clive had been accused of plagiarizing his ideas. And the amount of information about him was overwhelming. 'You can cut a novel by 250 pages, but how do you cut a life?' 'The facts', she wailed to Vita, 'the swarm of facts. How can anyone lift a pen among them!' But she was committed by her promise to the sisters. Somehow she would have to indicate his love-affairs without stressing them, for even Bloomsbury would not accept a treatment of sex in biography which became customary forty years later. To Ethel she wrote, 'How does one square the relatives? How does one euphemise 20 different mistresses? But Roger every day turns out more miraculous.'

She slowly recovered her health after the ordeal of *The Years*, and was able to alternate her literary work with other obligations, just as Leonard managed to combine progress with his magnum opus *After the Deluge* with control of the Hogarth Press. When Margaret West, the most satisfactory of their managers, died in 1937, their burden was doubled. Virginia was still the main reader of manuscripts submitted to them, and travelled their books on publication. As the Press became better known, and Virginia herself its star author, inevitably the flood of unsolicited prose and poetry increased. 'Every boy and girl who can buy a fountain pen and a ream of paper', she told Janet Case, 'instantly writes a novel, ties it up and sends it to us.' But she found time to write articles for the weekly journals, and gave one broadcast in the BBC series 'Words Fail Me'. The tape of her talk, which she called

Craftsmanship, is the only substantial recording of her voice that survives. It had a sing-song quality, a rise and fall in intonation, with emphasis placed in unexpected places, as in 'c*i*viliz*a*tion'. It was known as the Bloomsbury voice.

The abdication of Edward VIII in December 1936, before he had even been crowned, thrust aside for a few days every other consideration, personal and public. Virginia was excited to be living through an event which would be discussed for centuries to come. She did not much care for the monarchy. As a girl, she had stood in the street while Queen Victoria's carriage rolled by, but that was her nearest encounter with royalty. When George V died, she thought the public's grief 'for a very commonplace man' excessive. To her it was a curious survival of 'barbarism, emotionalism, heraldry, ecclesiasticism, sheer sentimentality and snobbery'. Of Edward VIII she wrote, from hearsay, that he was 'a cheap second-rate little bounder, whose only good points are that he keeps two mistresses and likes dropping into tea with the wives of miners', when there was only one current mistress, Wallis Simpson, and only one cup of tea with a miner's wife.

When the King's affair became public knowledge, Bloomsbury's attitude was one of liberal indifference. Why shouldn't he marry anyone he wants? But when they realized that the very existence of the monarchy, not just the fate of one monarch, was involved, they slightly changed their tune. This 'insignificant little man' was moving a pebble that could precipitate an avalanche. So let him keep Wallis as his mistress, and when he tires of her, take another. 'But apparently', Virginia noted in her diary, 'the King's little bourgeois demented mind sticks fast to the marriage service', in order to make

Wallis respectable at the cost of losing his throne.

On Abdication Day, 10 December 1936, she took a bus to Whitehall, where a shuffling crowd awaited the news. By chance she met Lady Ottoline there, and, inspired by the same reflections, they looked up at the window from which Charles I had stepped onto the scaffold. 'I felt I was walking in the 17th century with one of the courtiers, and she was lamenting not the abdication of Edward but the execution of Charles.' They hailed a taxi. The driver said, 'We don't want a woman that's already had two husbands, and an American, when there are so many good English girls.' *Vox populi.* Then they saw a newspaper van drive past bearing on its poster the one word ABDICATION.

XII

LIFE FOR THE WOOLFS returned to normal at the start of 1937, but international tensions were disturbing it. Leonard held constant meetings in Tavistock Square for politicians and journalists, from which, as far as she could manage, Virginia stood aloof. 'The bray and drone of those tortured voices almost sent me crazy', she wrote to Ethel, and having been persuaded to join a Committee of anti-Fascist intellectuals called Vigilance, she resigned, feeling that she had nothing to contribute. Leonard could speak for both of them. People were always asking her what she thought was happening in Abyssinia, in Poland, in Spain. She had no idea. 'Why does everyone bother me about politics?', she moaned to Ethel. 'Do you also have to trump up this meaningless nonsense, sign books, sign letters perpetually?' She was reserving her fire for *Three Guineas*.

Then something happened which forced her to pay attention. Julian Bell was killed in the Spanish Civil War.

Virginia was devoted to him and had come to admire him for his sterling character, and because they shared Vanessa between them. After his death she wrote privately, 'Our relationship was secure because it was founded on our passion – not too strong a word for either of us – for Nessa.' She liked his strong, masculine, adventurous style. He reminded her in some ways of her brother Thoby, who died at about the same age. They were both intellectuals in the sense that they were interested in ideas and the clear expression of them, but Thoby had been more mature in his thinking and writing than Julian, who 'never quite grew up', wrote Leonard. His life, like his writing, was never co-ordinated, although in love and politics he had lived it to the full. He had no profession, and no real qualifications for one. He had failed to gain a Fellowship at King's. The Hogarth Press had rejected his Memoir of Roger Fry, and T.S. Eliot (for Faber's) a collection of his essays. On his return from China in March 1937 Virginia saw in him a new maturity. He was well able to hold his own in political debate with Leonard and his father, but he was still excitable, clumsy (Keynes's word), undisciplined, though immensely likeable, combining in his character qualities inherited from both his parents, Clive's rumbustiousness, Vanessa's integrity. In looks he was a young Achilles.

Why did he decide, against the advice of his friends and

the entreaties of Vanessa and Virginia, to fight on the Republican side against Franco? Many of his contemporaries saw in the Spanish Civil War the stage on which the major political struggle of the period was being enacted, Communism versus Fascism. Julian was not a Communist. Surprisingly, indeed, he was not much interested in the ideological conflict. A friend, Richard Rees, who was in Spain with him, testified that 'political subtleties and allegiances did not overly concern him'. He was more attracted by the opportunity to experience war, to be 'in the thick of things', to prove his manhood, to strengthen his hold on life. After a somewhat fluttering youth, he yearned for excitement, perhaps glory. Virginia explained it as 'a fever in the blood'. It was also in reaction to Bloomsbury's pacifism. He would not be content to sit comfortably at Cambridge waging the intellectual battle when the only activity that mattered was at the front. But knowing how greatly he was distressing his mother, he agreed to compromise. He would not enlist as a soldier in the International Brigade. He would join a British unit, known as Spanish Medical Aid, as a non-combatant, and drive an ambulance. This would satisfy Bloomsbury's pacifism without allaying their fears for his safety.

He joined the unit in July on the eve of a major Republican offensive to relieve Franco's investment of Madrid. His role was to ferry casualties from the battlefield to two hospitals established in Philip II's great palace of the Escorial. Though his task was passive, it was highly dangerous. He was constantly under fire. Half the British medical unit were killed in the battle. On 18 July 1937 Julian himself was killed by a shell-splinter plunging deep into his chest. He was taken to the Escorial and died there six hours later. His last words were,

'Well, I always wanted a mistress and a chance to go to war, and now I've had both.'

The news reached England two days later, and for the next few weeks Virginia was constantly at her sister's side, first in London and then at Charleston, and she wrote to her every day when they were apart. It was not simply consolation that she offered, but her presence. She could not tell her sister what she thought, that Julian's death was a 'complete waste', as she said to others, and endeavoured to invest it with a certain grandeur. He had died doing what he wanted. It cannot have been easy for her. Her intimacy with Vanessa had never, since childhood, been fully reciprocated. 'When she is demonstrating I always shrink away', Vanessa once confessed. Now that an event so terrible, so deeply personal, had brought them closely together again, Virginia found not only words of sympathy which must soon have been exhausted, but an attitude, often expressed by silence, and then, as the pain lessened, by shared memories and jokes, which Vanessa could accept from no other person, least of all from Julian's father, Clive. Years later, after Virginia's death, she wrote to my mother, 'I remember all those days after I heard about Julian, lying in an unreal state and hearing her voice going on and on, keeping life going when otherwise it would have stopped.' At the time she found it impossible to express her gratitude to her sister. She asked Vita, whom she scarcely knew and did not much like, to express it for her. 'I cannot ever say how Virginia has helped me. Perhaps some day, not now, you will be able to tell her.' Vita passed on the message.

Julian's death coincided with Virginia's immersion in *Three Guineas*, a condemnation of war and of men who wage war.

To her it was agonizing that the young man of whom she was most deeply fond had thrown away his life in the manner that she most deeply deplored. She did not mention his fate to fortify her argument – indeed, there is nothing in any way autobiographical in the book – but 'I was always thinking of Julian when I wrote'. She was determined to expose the folly of resisting evil by a greater evil. It was a pacifist's statement, but it was something more. She wished to lay the blame for war on men and their treatment of women. She came near to saying that if women had a greater influence in the state, there would be no wars. They were denied that influence. They were poorly educated, excluded from the professions, and even given a subordinate place in the home. Women should protest, not militantly like Ethel Smyth, but passively. They should have no share in male arrogance and ambition. They must declare themselves 'outsiders', even to the extent of abrogating their nationality. 'If you insist on fighting to protect me or "our country",' she wrote, 'let it be understood soberly and rationally between us, that you are fighting to gratify a sex instinct which I cannot share; to procure benefits which I have not shared and probably will not share.' No appeal could be made to women to contribute to their country's defence, as their country had done nothing for them. The outsider will say, 'in fact, as a woman, I have no country. I want no country. As a woman my country is the whole world.' That was the pith of her argument. It was neither sober nor rational.

I find myself in some difficulty. I am writing the life of a woman for whom I had great affection and whom I much admired. I am obliged to argue against her profoundest convictions on a subject central to her life. In the Introductions to Volumes 5 and 6 of her Letters I stated my reasons, and find little need to alter them. Hermione Lee in her biography of Virginia said that I and others like me, including Quentin Bell, misunderstood and undervalued Virginia's attitude. She was tapping a deep well of feminine grievance in a profound and very vivid way. While *A Room of One's Own* had stated the case for women's rights charmingly, wittily, *Three Guineas* was angry. Much of it was written with a stridency that I do not recognize in any of her other books, her diary, her letters or her conversation. She considered that she had the right to be angry. It was her duty to exploit her fame as a vehicle for her protest. She was living in very dangerous times. They were dangerous, she thought, because men were instinctively bellicose. Men liked conflict: women didn't.

Nobody denies her right to say this, but her reasoning must be open to challenge. As Quentin Bell put it, 'It was wrong to involve a discussion of women's rights with the far more agonising and immediate question: What we were to do in order to meet the evergrowing menace of Fascism and war.' The two controversies had little in common. Nor was it true that women in general were more pacifist than men: from Helen of Troy to Margaret Thatcher they have encouraged war as an instrument of policy, and to demonstrate men's hardihood and pride. It was not other men in the First World War who distributed white feathers to supposed malingerers, but women. They admired the brave, despised the cowardly, and in later wars were proud to share its hazards with men. If Virginia was right, why were women not all pacifist? Why did they not use their new-won votes to overthrow any government that advocated war? And how did she propose to overcome Fascism, which she hated, except by military preparations to fight it?

It could be argued that as a pamphleteer – and she called *Three Guineas* 'my war pamphlet' – one should not expect from her a scholar's fidelity to logic and sources. She was not a politician. Leonard remarked in his autobiography that she was the most unpolitical person since Aristotle invented the term. But in *Three Guineas* she was using the weapons of political invective and the scholarly apparatus of quotation and extensive footnotes. She wished to be taken seriously, particularly on the theme which she had prefaced in *A Room of One's Own*, that women had always been disadvantaged by men, and still were. She was not complaining of her own fate, for the flowering of her genius had in no way been thwarted by ill-treatment or convention. It is true that she had been deprived of a university education, but that meant only that she had never experienced the intellectual discipline that might have saved her from the hyperbole of *Three Guineas*. As in *A Room* she was speaking only of women of her own class and cultural background, a tiny minority who had little cause for complaint. As I summed up my criticism of her argument in 1979: 'Today the newspapers print every day the obituaries of women who began distinguished careers at the very time when Virginia was protesting that few opportunities existed for them. She drew most of her examples from the past, but presented them in such a way as to suggest that they were still relevant. She was describing a world that had evaporated, but which to her was still real. She, who had won free from it so young, so defiantly, so successfully, was almost alone in imagining that nothing had basically changed.'

Three Guineas was published in June 1938, and was given a warm but not rapturous reception by the critics. Graham Greene and Basil de Selincourt were friendly, if a little puzzled, perhaps feeling nervous that if they picked holes in her arguments, they would be confirming everything that Virginia had written about male arrogance. Women were more outspoken. Theodora Bosanquet wrote in *Time and Tide*, 'I do not suppose that Mrs Woolf would sustain in the teeth of much evidence that jealousy, vanity, greed and possessiveness are found only in public life and exhibited almost exclusively by the male sex', and Queenie Leavis said in a long article which Virginia did not even bother to read to the end, that 'this book is not merely silly and ill-informed, but contains self-indulgent sex-hostility'.

At first Virginia did not mind these attacks. She expected them. She was proud of what she had done. 'I thought I would raise their hackles – poor old strumpets', she wrote in her diary after reading the first reviews. 'I have already gained my point, I am taken seriously, not dismissed as a charming prattler as I feared.' Nelly Cecil, Lady Rhondda (an ardent feminist), Naomi Mitchison, Emmeline Pethick Lawrence (the doyenne of the Women's Suffrage Movement) and of course Ethel Smyth ('Your book is so splendid that it makes me hot'), wrote her letters of gratitude for what she had done for their cause. Bloomsbury were slightly embarrassed by it. Keynes called it 'a silly argument, and not very well written', a verdict of which the first part could be defended but not the second, since it was eloquent and elegant in style and muscular in treatment. When Leonard first read it, 'he gravely approves' (Virginia's diary), and thinks it 'an extremely clear analysis', but that this was not his true opinion was revealed two months later when she noted, 'I didn't get so much praise from L. as I hoped', and significantly he made no comment on it in his Memoirs. As late as December 1938 she recorded, 'Not one of my friends has mentioned it' (not true), 'My wide circle has widened, but I am altogether in the dark as to the true merits of the book.'

Curiously it was Vita who aroused her to protest. She had written to Virginia, 'You are a tantalising writer because at one moment you enchant one with your lovely prose and next moment exasperate one with your misleading arguments. I read you with delight, even though I wanted to exclaim, "Oh but Virginia", on 50 per cent of your pages.' Virginia replied, 'When you say that you are exasperated by my "misleading arguments", I ask, What do you mean? If I said, I don't agree with your conception of Joan of Arc's character [in Vita's recent book about her], that's one thing. But if I said, Your arguments about her are "misleading", shouldn't I mean, Vita has cooked the facts in a dishonest way in order to produce an effect which she knows to be untrue?' Unfortunately that came close to expressing exactly what Vita did mean, as is shown by her own copy of *Three Guineas*, which is scored with exclamation marks and hostile annotations. But she replied 'I never for a moment questioned your facts, but only disagreed in some places with the deductions you drew from them. ... To take an example, you suggest that fighting is a sex characteristic which women cannot share, but is it not true that many women are extremely bellicose and urge their men to fight?' Virginia did not reply to this. It was her only quarrel with Vita, and it left no permanent scar.

XIII

THE HOGARTH PRESS was still extending its scope without growing to a size that would have monopolized their time or exposed it to a takeover bid from larger publishers. In 1938 John Lehmann, after a brief absence, became an equal partner with Leonard, buying out Virginia's half-share for £3,000 and bringing with him the literary miscellany *New Writing* which he had founded and edited and was ideally suited to the Press's tradition. At first the partnership was an uneasy one. When the agreement was signed, Lehmann proposed that they should celebrate the event by drinking a toast, but Leonard grimly replied that he had only cold water in which to drink it. Then Virginia turned down Lehmann's own novel, and they disagreed about the memorial volume of Julian's poetry and essays which Quentin was editing. No wonder that Virginia complained to Vanessa, 'John is as touchy as a very old spinster whose one evening dress has a hole in the behind', but it was as much Leonard's reluctance to share control as John's touchiness which caused the trouble. However, Lehmann remained Leonard's partner until 1946, when he left to found his own publishing firm.

Looking back, the Hogarth Press had been a great success. Its history has been admirably written by Professor J.H. Willis of William and Mary College, Williamsburg, and in his concluding chapter he draws up a balance sheet, regarding it first as a business, then as a contribution to English culture. It was not until 1928, when they published thirty-six titles, that the annual profit exceeded £100. It rose to a peak in 1930 with

£2,373 (*The Edwardians* year) and to £2,442 in 1937 with *The Years*. Virginia and Vita, and Sigmund Freud, were undoubtedly the main money-spinners. As for the quality of its output, Willis is fully justified in concluding that 'Virginia Woolf's nine major works of fiction and non-fiction, T.S. Eliot's two volumes of poetry, translations of Freud's eight best-known books and the translations of Rilke's poetry in five volumes would make the Hogarth Press an important publisher even if it published nothing else.' In Virginia's lifetime they published 474 volumes, an impressive contribution to the intellectual life of England between the wars, but surprisingly they had not been able to attract the major Bloomsbury authors apart from Virginia herself. Forster, Strachey, Keynes and Fry were under contract to larger publishers, and Eliot and Plomer abandoned them once the Woolfs had made them famous. It was only out of loyalty to Leonard that Virginia played so large a part for so long, and the emergence of John Lehmann as a partner was a great relief to them both.

Two months after his appointment, they went on holiday to Scotland. It was Virginia's only visit there apart from a brief trip to Glasgow in 1913. On their drive north they discovered parts of England which she imagined they were the first people ever to explore, particularly the more desolate parts of Northumberland where Hadrian's Wall runs across the moors. 'What the Romans saw, I see', she wrote, 'miles and miles of lavender-covered loneliness.' In the Highlands she was impressed, as she had been in Ireland, by the emptiness of the land and the poverty of the people, and sudden glimpses of Landseer scenes: 'There was one lake, with trees reflected, which I think carried beauty to the extreme point: whether it is expressible, that rapture, I doubt', but she was writing to Ethel. When writing to Vanessa she curbed expressions of her delight, thinking that Vanessa's tastes had far surpassed Landseers and that ecstasy of this sort would bore her.

On their return to Sussex, Virginia was involved in the continuing repercussions of *Three Guineas*, and she again took up, simultaneously, her two new books, the life of Roger Fry and *Pointz Hall* (published as *Between the Acts*.) She found the novel more enjoyable work than the biography, switching from 'assiduous truth' (Fry) to 'wild ideas' (*Pointz*). She was still worried how to deal with Fry's wife Helen, who was locked up mad, and his love-affair with Vanessa. 'What am I to say about you?', she asked her. Should she come out with the truth, or compromise? 'Do give me some views: how to deal with love so that we're not all blushing.' Vanessa replied, 'I hope you won't mind making us all blush. It won't do any harm, and anyhow, no one's blushes last long. ... The only important thing is to tell the truth, for the sake of the younger generation.' Despite this unexceptionable Bloomsbury declaration, Virginia did compromise. In the book she primly referred to the Vanessa–Roger relationship as 'their friendship'.

It was like handling three saucepans on the stove simultaneously. Fry and *Pointz* were alternately brought to the boil, while *Three Guineas* was left to simmer. It was the latter that caused her most trouble, both for the flood of reviews and letters that it provoked, and because actuality caught up with theory: how was she to respond to the imminence of another European war?

In 1936 she had allowed herself to become involved in a movement called 'For Intellectual Liberty', or FIL. Its membership was very select (Huxley, Wells, Forster, G.E. Moore, Gilbert Murray, Leonard Woolf), but its aims were uncertain, for it proclaimed 'the need for united action in defence of peace, liberty and culture', without agreeing on what that action should be beyond a vague appeal to governments to disarm and sign a universal treaty of peace. In face of Mussolini's conquest of Abyssinia and Hitler's occupation of the Rhineland and Austria, and the involvement of both dictators in the Spanish Civil War, such high-minded manifestos seemed an inadequate response. Were Britain and France to arm or disarm? Resist the dictators or surrender to them? Aldous Huxley, the President of FIL and an outright pacifist, resigned with the excuse that he intended to live in America, and Leonard, his deputy, was on the point of resignation for the opposite reason, that he was unable to persuade FIL or the Labour Party – he was still Secretary to its International Committee – to support rearmament as the only reaction that would make the dictators pause. 'Until the hawk actually has its beak in their flesh', he groaned, 'they will not face them.' The Tories were even worse. 'They do a dirty deal with Musso, and call it peace', he had written to Julian Bell in his most Tacitean manner. We should revert to rapid rearmament and a broad anti-Fascist alliance, including an Anglo-Soviet military pact. The great powers must unite to protect the smaller powers. This was Leonard's constant theme in the later 1930s and the message of his book *The Barbarians at the Gate*. It consorted ill with *Three Guineas*, where Virginia had declared herself an outsider who would have nothing to do with this masculine folly.

It was a difficult situation for her. The two main interests in her life – support for Leonard, and opposition to his most cherished beliefs – had come into conflict. She co-signed a letter to *The Times* appealing for 'sympathetic benevolence' towards the Spanish democrats, and a FIL telegram to the Prime Minister, Neville Chamberlain, which read, 'Profoundly deplore rapprochement Mussolini before his troops leave Spain'. This was safe enough. Neither sentiment involved rearmament. Her true feelings were expressed in a letter to Janet Case written from Monk's House on Christmas Eve 1936:

> I'm sitting over a log fire with Leonard reading history for his book [*After the Deluge*], and the black and white spaniel is in its basket beside him. I'm glad to hoick him away from his eternal meetings – Labour Party, Fabian Research, Intellectual Liberty, Spanish Medical Aid – oh dear, how they poach on him – what hours he spends with dirty, unkempt, ardent, ugly, entirely unpractical but no doubt well meaning philanthropists at whom I should throw the coal-scuttle after 10 minutes if I were in his place.

Franco's victory in Spain effectively put an end to FIL, and Virginia tried to face realities. At first she passed Hitler off as 'a ridiculous little man', and his speeches, which resounded by radio through the garden at Rodmell, as the ravings of a lunatic. Then the Munich Pact caught her in a dilemma. 'If it is war, then every country joins in: chaos. But it's a hopeless war this – when we know winning means nothing' (diary). But a week later: 'All Europe in Hitler's keeping. What'll he gobble next?' Like the great majority of her countrymen and women, she was ambivalent. How resist evil except by a greater evil? If Britain and France go to war to save

Czechoslovakia, would we carry our people with us? Would we win? Even Kingsley Martin, who almost camped on the Woolfs' doorstep during the crisis, came to the conclusion, 'the strategic value of the Bohemian frontier should not be made the occasion of a world war'. So the inglorious pact signed at Munich, which gave Hitler almost all he wanted (he took the rest), came as an intense relief. Virginia's letters to Vanessa, who was in France, described the sand-bagging, the trench-digging, the issue of gas masks, the plans to evacuate children from London, with a mixture of excitement and despair. When it was all over, she summed up her emotions for Ethel Smyth as a 'residue of anger and shame, on top of sheer cowardly relief'. Leonard considered that Munich meant 'peace without honour for six months'. It is not unfair to Virginia to conclude that she never clarified her mind. Pacifism, and with it the central argument of *Three Guineas*, had been overtaken by events. When war came a year later, and she expressed her horror, Leonard replied, 'Yes, but now it's come, it's better to win the war than lose it', to which Virginia had no reply. Wars can only be won by fighting.

Many friends and relations were dying before war added to their number. After Lytton, Carrington and Roger Fry, she lost George Duckworth, Ka Arnold-Forster, Janet Case, Charles Sanger, Mark Gertler (suicide), Leonard's mother, Jack Hills and (on the same day) Mitz the marmoset. She still needed the excitements of London. From time to time she complained of the 'frizz and fritter' of social life, but even lunch with Lady Colefax could be enjoyable. Colefax was ruthless in her head-hunting and earned the ridicule of her guests, but her parties were carefully composed, to the extent of excluding spouses whom she found uninteresting. On one

Roger Fry, a self-portrait now in the National Portrait Gallery. Virginia loved him for the three qualities that she emphasised in her biography of him, 'his charm, his intelligence, and his persistence, which in combination made him a major influence on his generation. He lifted people's spirits.'

such occasion, in November 1938, Virginia found herself in company with Max Beerbohm, Somerset Maugham and Christopher Isherwood, and she was careful to record her impressions of them, first in her diary, and then, sharpened, for Vanessa. Beerbohm was 'a charmer, rubicund, gay, apparently innocent but in fact very astute and full of airy fantasies'. Maugham was 'a grim figure, rat-eyed, dead-man cheeked, unshaven, a criminal I should have said had I met him in a bus'. Isherwood 'seemed all agog with amusement, but is a shifty, quick-silver little slip of a creature – very nimble and rather inscrutable and on his guard'. On leaving, Maugham said to her, indicating Isherwood, 'that young man holds the future of the English novel in his hands', a somewhat tactless statement that Virginia seems not to have taken amiss.

She also met Sigmund Freud. The Hogarth Press had been his British publishers since 1924, and now he was a refugee from Austria, living in Hampstead where the Woolfs called on him for tea in January 1939. The visit was not a great success. Virginia described him as 'a screwed up, shrunk, very old man [only 82], with a monkey's light eyes, paralysed spasmodic movements, inarticulate, alert'. He had an old-world courtesy (he solemnly presented Virginia with a narcissus), and Leonard's impression was of 'great gentleness, but behind the gentleness, great strength'. They never saw him again. He died from cancer eight months later.

Bloomsbury was diminishing in importance in Virginia's life. Her main correspondents were still Ethel Smyth, Vanessa and Vita, and it was curiously Vita's elder son, Ben, who after the outbreak of war caused her to write him a careful retrospect of its significance. Ben had rather foolishly attacked Bloomsbury, and Fry in particular, for its ineffectual stance against Fascism and social injustice. They had been living in 'a fool's paradise', he wrote to Virginia. She was fond of Ben, and had asked him to sort out some of Fry's papers. She answered him in two long letters, for one of which she made a rare draft that also survives, protesting that Bloomsbury had done its best. Keynes had written *The Economic Consequences of the Peace*; Leonard had alerted us for years to the menace of the dictators; she herself had worked at Morley College and for Women's Suffrage, and had written *Three Guineas*. What more could they have done? Lytton by his books, Duncan and Vanessa by their paintings, Roger by his lectures, had opened people's eyes to new ideas and roused them from cultural apathy. Should they have become active politicians? What was Ben himself doing about it? He was an art historian, and Deputy Surveyor of the Kings's Pictures under Kenneth Clark. Was his occupation any less ivory-tower than Fry's had been? Artists do not, cannot, influence events, she said. They must use their gifts to widen understanding and appreciation of the arts. But what's the use of telling people who left school at the age of fourteen that they ought to enjoy Shakespeare? She had just been lecturing to a working-class audience at Brighton, and sensed a gulf that was almost unbridgeable, but it was not for that reason a matter for shame. Her replies to Ben were more tolerant and logical than his attack, though clearly she was indignant. It was typical of her to end her letter by inviting him to spend his leave at Rodmell.

Her main defence of Bloomsbury and its values was her biography of Roger Fry, published in July 1940. She had not enjoyed the heavy breathing of the Fry family down her neck as she was writing it, and she was not practised in biography.

Nor did she enjoy the advantages enjoyed by the biographer of, say, Virginia Woolf, for whom the main work has already been done by others, the diaries annotated, the letters collected, the arguments for and against astutely marshalled. But she had known her subject intimately, been intimate with his intimates, and had loved him for the three qualities that she chose to emphasize, his charm, his intelligence and his persistence, which in combination had made him a major influence on his generation. Virginia quoted with approval Julian Bell's comment, 'He made one share his pleasure in thinking', which might be taken as a tribute to Bloomsbury as a whole. He lifted people's spirits, as when he persuaded businessmen to accept Omega products, telling them, 'It is time that the spirit of fun was introduced into furniture and fabrics. We have suffered too long from the dull and the stupidly serious', or when addressing a wider public at the time of the Post-Impressionist exhibitions, he said, according to Virginia, that 'he feared that the art of painting was circling purposelessly among frivolities and was at a dead end. Now he was convinced that it was alive, and that a great age was at hand.' Virginia's description of Fry's personality and life, sometimes introducing her own memories of him, but only in the third person ('a friend', 'an admirer'), was alternately taut with meaning or running fresh with pleasure. The review of the book that she most appreciated was by J.T. Sheppard, where he said that Roger Fry was there and not Virginia Woolf. But Leonard was frankly critical. The book was too impersonal, he told her: 'It's merely analysis, not history'. It was the first time that he had ever directly criticized her work. In moments of depression, she considered that it was not a book at all, but 'cabinet making'.

XIV

THE WOOLFS NEVER denied themselves an annual holiday however pressing their work, and in June 1939 they toured Normandy and Brittany by car, finding renewed pleasure in non-English sights like a pale farmhouse disguised as a château or a bishop blessing a fishing-boat. On their return to London they were obliged to leave 52 Tavistock Square, where they had lived for fifteen years, because it was due to be demolished (a fate anticipated in 1940 by German bombs), and move to a flat in 37 Mecklenburgh Square, only a few blocks away, taking the Hogarth Press and its files with them. The move was not completed until after the outbreak of war, which considerably hampered it, and they were not able to occupy even a single room until October.

Virginia was completing her revision of *Roger Fry* at the same time as Leonard published the second volume of his *After the Deluge*, and she was also writing articles and stories for American magazines, including one of her best-known, 'Lappin and Lapinova'. Although they were by now quite comfortably off, the Woolfs were nervous about overspending on small luxuries ('Should I spend 1/8 on scissors?', Virginia asked herself) or on loans to other people. It was this constant need to top up their income – for Leonard earned very little – that accounts for Virginia's remarkable output of journalism. One tends to think of her as a novelist who published a new book once every four or five years, but her critical essays filled three posthumous volumes, apart from *The Common Reader*, First and Second Series published in her lifetime, and her shorter fiction occupies a stout volume. In addition, the Hogarth Press issued in the autumn of 1939 her pamphlet *Reviewing*, and having refused the prestigious Clark lectures at Cambridge, she spent weeks preparing for the Brighton branch of the Workers' Educational Association a lecture on modern literature, later published as 'The Leaning Tower'. *Pointz Hall*, for the moment, was set aside. She also began to write her Memoirs, but they made little progress before she died.

Britain and France declared war on Germany on 3 September 1939, when they were at Monk's House, and they remained there for most of the winter, one of the coldest on record, with occasional trips to London. At first Virginia felt only 'dumb rage' at being 'fought for by young people whom one wants to see making love'. Although the war entered an inactive phase between the conquest of Poland and the German invasion of Norway in April 1940, she was unable to isolate herself from it. London children and pregnant mothers were evacuated to Rodmell (but not to Monk's House), clerks from the Hogarth Press took it in turn to spend quiet weekends there, the village windows were blacked out to hide from German pilots signs of inhabited places, and there were weekly meetings of the Labour Party to discuss the latest events. It seemed at times, as Virginia wrote to Ethel Smyth, that 'there's a peace in the country which surrounds me as a mouse is surrounded by cheese' but in London, she recorded in her diary, 'You never escape the war. Very few buses. Tubes closed. No children. No loitering. Everyone humped with a gas-mask. Strain and grimness. At night it's so verdurous and gloomy that one expects a badger or a fox to prowl along the pavement. A reversion to the middle ages with all the space and silence of the country set in this forest of black houses.'

There was scarcely a single air raid during that first winter of war, and no fighting on land. Virginia wrote to Vita, 'Of course I'm not in the least patriotic', but she let drop phrases to other people which indicated that she was not in the least indifferent either. To Eddy Sackville-West, for example, she wrote of 'the obvious horror we all feel for war; but then, with a solid block of unbaked barbarians in Germany, what's the good of our being comparatively civilised?'; and to Judith Stephen, Adrian's young daughter, 'I'm more and more convinced that it is our duty to catch Hitler in his home haunts and prod him if even with only the end of an old inky pen.' The pen was hers; but the 'catching' could only be by air attack. Bloomsbury was no longer pacifist. Even Clive Bell patrolled the South Downs with a slung rifle. Only Ham Spray, where Frances Partridge kept the flag of pacifism flying with her husband Ralph, was faithful to the cause, and this was all the more remarkable, because Ralph had fought with the utmost gallantry in the First War. His experience was his main reason for thinking its successor ethically unjustifiable.

When a significant event occurred in the outside world, like the sinking of a great ship or the Russian invasion of Finland, Virginia mentioned it casually in her diary after noting that she had seen a kingfisher on her walk. Her mood was melancholy and subdued, further depressed by an acute attack of influenza in March. Then in May 1940 it was no longer possible for anyone to lead a sheltered life. The German army swept through France, the British escaped without their weapons from Dunkirk, and were evicted from Norway. In

her diary of 25 May she made a rare strategic judgment, not far short of the truth: 'The Germans seem youthful, fresh, inventive. We plod behind.' In her letters she barely referred to these disasters, just as Jane Austen, writing to her sister from their brother's house near Canterbury, never mentioned Napoleon's army poised for invasion from Boulogne. But in her diary she kept an almost day-by-day record of her experiences and reactions, and it is interesting to see how her mood varied with the intensity of the crisis. In July she wrote, 'I don't like any of the feelings that war breeds: patriotism; all sentimental and emotional parodies of real feelings', and when she saw soldiers passing through Sussex after escaping from France, she thought it absurd to describe them as heroes. But during the air battles over south-east England, of which she was often a direct witness – even falling flat on her face in the garden of Monk's House when German planes flew so low that she could see the swastika painted on their tail fins – she felt a stirring of hatred for them. Watching a squadron of British fighters flying out to sea to intercept a Luftwaffe raid, she wrote, 'I almost instinctively wished them luck', as if surprised by her emotion. At that moment, she was glad that she was of the same race as them. For Churchill she could not suppress a certain admiration. 'A clear, measured, robust speech', she commented when he spoke of the imminence of invasion. It was natural for her to identify love of the Sussex

Virginia Woolf in 1939, a photograph taken, much against her will, by Gisèle Freund. She wrote to Vita: 'I'm in a rage. That devil woman Giselle [sic] Freund calmly tells me that she's showing those d—d photographs – and I made it a condition she shouldn't. I loathe being hoisted about on top of a stick for anyone to stare at.' In fact, it is the best photograph ever taken of her.

countryside with love of England, and to that extent she reversed what she had told Vita, that she had not a grain of patriotism in her. London, too, raked her heart. 'Have you that feeling for certain alleys and little courts between Chancery Lane and the City?', she asked Ethel. 'I walked to the Tower the other day by way of caressing my love of all that.' She felt for ordinary people an affinity that she had scarcely acknowledged before. In September 1940 she wrote, again to Ethel:

> When I see a great smash like a crushed matchbox where an old house stood, I wave my hand to London. What I'm finding odd and agreeable and unwonted is the admiration this war creates – for every sort of person: chars, shopkeepers, even much more remarkably, for politicians – Winston at least – and the tweed-wearing, sterling, dull women here [Rodmell], with their grim good sense. ... I'd almost lost faith in human beings, partly owing to my immersion in the dirty water of artists' envies and vanities while I worked at Roger. Now hope revives again.

At the height of the invasion threat, the Woolfs moved regularly between London and the country. Rodmell was only three miles from Newhaven, one of the south-coast ports where British Intelligence expected the Germans to land (correctly – it was the *Schwerpunkt* of their 9th Army, and paratroops would have dropped on the Downs), and Leonard, knowing that if they were captured, they would both be proscribed by the Gestapo for his Jewishness and prominent anti-Nazi activities, carried a lethal dose of morphine for both of them and kept enough petrol in his garage to asphyxiate themselves if the Germans landed. Yet they remained remarkably cool. Leonard wrote in his auto-biography, 'I never myself felt, or saw anyone else feeling, fear', and although I, who lived through the same period, find this statement scarcely credible, it is true that Virginia saw some beauty and excitement in the air battles overhead. 'It's rather lovely', she wrote to John Lehmann, 'to see the [search] lights stalking the Germans over the marshes', and when bombs breached the banks of the River Ouse, allowing the flood water to spread as far as Monk's House itself, she did not speculate that this would make invasion at this point less likely, but was reminded by it of William Morris's poem 'The Haystack in the Floods'. When four bombs flowered like ruby tulips in the nearby fields, she boasted that Vanessa, immune at Charleston, would be jealous.

It was during that long spring and summer of 1940 that *Roger Fry* was published, and it sold slowly, the military crisis making men like Fry seem somehow irrelevant. Virginia resumed her work on *Pointz Hall*, which at one moment she described as 'so much more of a strain than Roger', but on finishing it in November, she wrote in her diary, 'I've enjoyed writing almost every page'. There had been nothing to match the stress of *The Years*. She even found domestic chores enjoyable. Having lost her only live-in maid, she discovered for the first time the freedom that came from being unmolested by servants, and began to cook their meagre rations, helped by a village woman, Louie Everest, who remained with Leonard years after Virginia's death. She also joined the village Women's Institute and became its treasurer. It was a curiously pleasant existence, varied only by occasional visits to London and expeditions like that with Vita to Penshurst Place on the day when Paris fell. Sometimes visitors came for the night –

the MacCarthys, G.E. Moore, Elizabeth Bowen.

While Mecklenburgh Square was still intact, it was possible for them to stay there for a night or two. In September a bomb shattered a house across the street from their own, and another, unexploded, prevented them from approaching it. When it went off ten days later, the ceilings of No. 37 fell in, and the flat was uninhabitable. In October it was the turn of 52 Tavistock Square. It was flattened, Duncan's murals hanging over a smoking gap, but this was no cause for added distress, since they had failed to sublet the house and were still paying rent for it. Now it was impossible to charge for a house that did not exist. 'With a sigh of relief', wrote Virginia, 'we saw a heap of ruins.'

With the greatest difficulty they moved their belongings from Mecklenburgh to the country, climbing over the fallen plaster to retrieve their sodden books and papers, and they rented some rooms in Rodmell where they could temporarily store them. John Lehmann moved the Hogarth Press and its staff to Letchworth in Hertfordshire, where the Woolfs visited him in February 1941. But it was at Monk's House that Virginia spent the remaining months of her life, and they were the months when the German *Blitzkrieg* slackened. They lived in comparative peace. Virginia's feminist instincts resurfaced. In a lecture to the village branch of the Labour Party on Women and War, she argued that wars derived from 'manliness' and manliness bred 'womanliness' – 'both so hateful', she wrote to Lady Simon, 'but I was scowled at as a prostitute'.

Those same village people, in disguise, were the characters in *Pointz Hall*, which she renamed in the last stages of revision as *Between the Acts*. In the novel she attempted to mingle history with reality, the events occupying a single day as in

Mrs Dalloway but reaching back for centuries as in *Orlando*. This device was made possible by making a village pageant the central episode of the book, with scenes acted by the villagers. In amateurish make-believe they depicted the English character from the time of Queen Elizabeth to the present day. The novel was as ambitious as the pageant itself. It was the only time when Virginia attempted to mingle ancient forms of dialogue with modern rustic speech, and to portray the interpenetration of classes from the owners of Pointz Hall, where the pageant was staged, to the village idiot. The novel had a deeper meaning too. She was exploring the spiritual significance of life, and how it came about that civilization had been created by such trivial characters as ourselves. Her message was as puzzling to her readers as the pageant was to its audience. Perhaps Virginia was aware of this. It is known that she intended to revise it further. Conceivably she might have toned down the comedy to reveal the tragedy more clearly, and made more obvious when her characters were speaking as themselves or as symbols. We cannot be sure. The book was published by Leonard after her death with the cautious note: 'She would not, I believe, have made any large or material alterations.'

XV

ON 25 JANUARY 1941 Virginia Woolf reached the age of fifty-nine. She did not suffer from the usual infirmities of advancing age, like deafness or loss of memory, and although she told several people that her hands had begun to tremble, there is no sign of this in her manuscripts, which remained clear and distinguished till the end. Her letters were cheerful, and those she wrote to Vita were specially affectionate, as if she was appealing for a renewal of their love: 'How I long to hear from your own lips what's been worrying you – for you'll never shake me off – no!' 'How much I depend on you, and should mind any word that annoyed or hurt you.' Again: 'What can one say – except that I love you, and I've got to live through this strange quiet evening thinking of you sitting alone.' They were reunited by the experience of the war, their neighbour-counties, Sussex and Kent, being the most vulnerable to invasion and the skies above them scarred by the same planes in combat. Vita once managed to make the journey to Rodmell in spite of petrol rationing. On 17 February she spent a night there, and lectured to the village Women's Institute on her journeys to Persia. It was the last time that the two women met.

Almost to the end Virginia was capable of much enjoyment and intensive work. After her death Leonard discovered as many as eight drafts of a review she had written of a biography of Mrs Thrale, her last piece of criticism, and while revising *Between the Acts*, she was also toying with *Anon*, her history of literature. She was enjoying her household chores – making butter, beating carpets, arranging books – and visitors saw little change in her manner. This was Elizabeth Bowen's recollection of a two-night visit in February: 'I remember her kneeling back on the floor – we were tacking away, mending a torn Spanish curtain in the house – and she sat back on her heels, and put her head back in a patch of sun, early spring sun. Then she laughed in this consuming, choking, delightful, hooting way. That is what has remained with me.'

Her diary offers some more sombre clues. On 26 January she wrote that she was 'in a trough of despair', but it seemed short-lived; and on 8 March she wrote of 'my despondency', but 'I shall conquer this mood, and I will go down with flying colours'. Various things contributed to her depression. The war, of course, and the renewed threat of invasion in the spring; the destruction of her two London homes; the rationing of basic foods; the difficulty of travel; Angelica's love-affair with David Garnett (whom she later married), which Virginia considered 'grotesque' given their disparity in age. More important was her fear of failure as a writer. Leonard's criticism of *Roger Fry* may still have rankled, but it was mainly *Between the Acts* that worried her. She thought it foolish, not worth publishing. She told her new doctor, Octavia Wilberforce, at the end of December that it was 'a completely worthless book', and her disappointment with it never left her during the remaining months of her life. Although Leonard genuinely praised the book, thinking it 'better than anything she has written', as he told her American publisher, Donald Brace, Virginia was insistent that it needed extensive revision, if not cancelling altogether. This was not merely her usual reaction on finishing a book. It was something more terrible. She sensed a decline in her creative energy. 'I've lost all power over words', she told Dr Wilberforce, 'can't do a thing with them.' What was the point of living if she was never again to understand the shape of the world around her, or be able to describe it? In any case, who cared about books in wartime? 'It's difficult, I find, to write', she told another friend. 'No audience. No private stimulus, only this outer roar.' To end her life at this point was like ending a book: it had a certain artistic integrity.

It is only in retrospect that her intimates recognized the signs of approaching disaster. Vanessa 'never suspected the danger'. Vita and Ethel Smyth thought her no more affected by the war than they all were, and her letters gave them no other clue. Leonard in his autobiography said that he 'had no foreboding until the beginning of 1941', and that it was not until 25 January that she showed the 'first symptoms of serious mental disturbance'. She had begun to hear voices. She ate but little. She was advised by Dr Wilberforce, who had become her closest confidante, that she should stop working for a space: she needed rest, and as far as wartime rationing allowed, a proper diet. Virginia would not heed these warnings. She sensed that she was going mad again, and although she well knew that rest had cured her before, she was convinced that she would never recover this time. It was better to die while she was sane than linger on as a burden to others. But there was nobody with whom she could discuss it. If she opened her heart to Leonard, Vanessa or even Wilberforce, they would put her under constraints to prevent her harming herself. She must escape them, and face them with the accomplished fact.

She left three suicide notes behind her. Joanne Trautmann and I brooded over them for a long time (the originals are in the British Library), and came to a conclusion different from Leonard's and Quentin Bell's, who believed that she had written all three on the day of her suicide. We concluded from the evidence of the letters themselves that she had first attempted to kill herself on 18 March 1941. She arrived back at Monk's House dripping wet, and told Leonard that she had fallen by accident into a water-filled ditch. He had not found the letter that she had left for him, and suspected nothing. It was the most significant of the three, and I give it in full:

Tuesday

Dearest, I feel certain that I am going mad again: I feel we cant go through another of those terrible times. And I shant recover this time. I begin to hear voices, and cant concentrate. So I am doing what seems the best thing to do. You have given me the greatest possible happiness. You have been in every way all that anyone could be. I dont think two people could have been happier till this terrible disease came. I cant fight it any longer, I know that I am spoiling your life, that without me you could work. And you will I know. You see I cant even write this properly. I cant read. What I want to say is that I owe all the happiness of my life to you. You have been entirely patient with me and incredibly good. I want to say that – everybody knows it. If anybody could have saved me it would have been you. Everything has gone from me but the certainty of your goodness. I cant go on spoiling your life any longer.

I dont think two people could have been happier than we have been.

After writing this letter, she lived another ten days. In her diary, which she continued to write until 24 March, there was no hint of what she had done or intended to do. She wrote a similar letter to Vanessa, but hid it with her first letter to Leonard, and simulated calm. Although Leonard was aware that she might be on the verge of a major breakdown, he reasoned that if he bothered her, or appeared to be monitoring her every movement, he might drive her to take the very action that non-interference might avert. He did, however, persuade her, much against her will, to visit Dr Wilberforce in Brighton on 27 March, but nothing much resulted from the consultation. Wilberforce said afterwards that she foresaw no immediate danger and counselled Virginia, once again, to rest. On the same day Virginia wrote to John Lehmann telling him not to publish *Between the Acts*: 'it's too silly and trivial'.

Next morning, Friday 28 March 1941, she went as usual to her garden lodge, and having spent some time there alone, she wrote a second, shorter, letter to Leonard, repeating the sense of the first. Leaving it in the lodge, she took her two earlier letters into the house and put them where Leonard would find them. Then, about midday, she walked the half-mile to the River Ouse, and thrusting a large stone into the pocket of her fur coat, she threw herself into the water. Although she could swim, she forced herself to drown. It must have been a terrifying death.

Leonard, on discovering her notes, searched the river bank and saw her walking-stick floating on the surface, but no sign of her. There was little doubt what had happened. He told Vanessa, who by chance called at Monk's House that afternoon, and wrote one letter, to Vita: 'I do not want you to see in the paper or hear possibly on the wireless the terrible thing that has happened to Virginia...'.

Vita hoped that they would never find her body: 'I hope that it will be carried out to sea.' But three weeks later it was found by some children who thought it was a floating log washed up by the bridge at Southease, not far from the place where she had drowned herself. After the inquest, she was cremated at Brighton, with only Leonard as a witness, and her ashes were interred in the garden at Rodmell, with the last words of *The Waves* as her epitaph:

> Against you I will fling myself unvanquished
> and unyielding, O Death.

SHORT BIBLIOGRAPHY

Books by Virginia Woolf

The Voyage Out. 1915
Night and Day. 1919
Jacob's Room. 1922
Mrs Dalloway. 1925
The Common Reader (First Series). 1925
To the Lighthouse. 1927
Orlando: A Biography. 1928
A Room Of One's Own. 1929
The Waves. 1931
The Common Reader (Second Series). 1932
Flush: A Biography. 1933
The Years. 1937
Three Guineas. 1938
Roger Fry: A Biography. 1940
Between the Acts. 1941, posthumously

All of the above titles, except the first two, published by the Hogarth Press. *The Voyage Out* and *Night and Day* published by Duckworth's.

The Diary of Virginia Woolf, edited in five volumes by Anne Olivier Bell, assisted by Andrew McNeillie. 1977–84, Hogarth Press

The Letters of Virginia Woolf, edited in six volumes by Nigel Nicolson and Joanne Trautmann. 1975–80, Hogarth Press

Congenial Spirits. The Selected Letters of Virginia Woolf, edited by Joanne Trautmann Banks. 1989, Hogarth Press

A Passionate Apprentice. The Early Journals 1897–1909, edited by Mitchell A. Leaska. 1990, Hogarth Press

Autobiography by Leonard Woolf, in five volumes (differently titled). 1960–69, Hogarth Press

Letters of Leonard Woolf, edited by Frederic Spotts. 1989, Weidenfeld & Nicolson

Moments of Being, edited by Jeanne Schulkind (memoirs by Virginia Woolf). 1985, Sussex University Press

Bell, Quentin: *Virginia Woolf, A Biography*, in two volumes. 1972, Hogarth Press *Elders and Betters*. 1995, John Murray

Bell, Vanessa: *Selected Letters*, edited by Regina Marler. 1993, Bloomsbury

Holroyd, Michael: *Lytton Strachey: The New Biography*. 1994, Chatto & Windus

Leaska, Mitchell A.: *Granite and Rainbow: The Hidden Life of Virginia Woolf*. 1998, Picador

Lee, Hermione: *Virginia Woolf*. 1996, Chatto & Windus

Lehmann, John: *Thrown to the Woolfs*. 1978, Weidenfeld & Nicolson

Sackville-West, Vita: *Letters to Virginia Woolf*, edited by Mitchell A. Leaska and Louise de Salvo. 1992, Hutchinson

Spalding, Frances: *Vanessa Bell.* 1983, Weidenfeld & Nicolson
    Duncan Grant. 1997, Chatto & Windus
Shone, Richard: *Bloomsbury Portraits.* 1976 and 1993, Phaidon
    Press *The Art of Bloomsbury.* 1999, Tate Gallery
Willis, J.H.: *Leonard and Virginia Woolf as Publishers.* 1992,
    University Press of Virginia